Managing a Quality Environment for IT
- Auditing and Cleaning

IT Infrastructure Library

Chris Kiddle
Paul Appleby

Riverwalk House
157-161 Millbank
LONDON, SW1P 4RT

London: HMSO

© Crown Copyright 1994

Applications for reproduction should be made to HMSO

First published   1994
ISBN   0 11 330574 5
ISSN   0956-2591

This is one of the books in the IT Infrastructure Library series. At regular intervals, further books will be published and the Library will be completed in 1994. Since many customers would like to receive the IT Infrastructure Library books automatically on publication, a standing order service has been set up. For further details on standing orders please contact:

HMSO Publicity (PU23 E3), FREEPOST,
Norwich, NR3 1BR
(*No stamp needed for UK customers*).

Until the whole Library is published, and subject to availability, draft copies of unpublished books may be obtained from CCTA if you are a standing order customer. To obtain drafts please contact:

IT Infrastructure Management Services
CCTA
Gildengate House, Upper Green Lane,
NORWICH, NR3 1DW.

For further information on other CCTA products, contact:

Press and Publications,
Room 3/9
CCTA
Gildengate House,
Upper Green Lane,
NORWICH, NR3 1DW.

This document has been produced using procedures conforming to
BS 5750 Part 1: 1987; ISO 9001: 1987.

Table of contents

1.	**Management summary**	**1**
2.	**Introduction**	**5**
2.1	Purpose of module	5
2.2	Target readership	5
2.3	Scope	5
2.4	Related guidance	7
2.5	Referenced documents	8
2.6	Definitions	8
2.7	Responsibilities	8
2.8	Relationships	8
3.	**Audit design and management**	**13**
3.1	Introduction	13
3.2	Preparing for the first audit	13
3.3	Executing the audit	16
3.4	Interpretation and follow-up action	16
3.5	Preparation for second and subsequent audits	18
4.	**Auditing computer accommodation**	**19**
4.1	Introduction	19
4.2	Legislation, standards and guidance	19
4.3	Scope and conduct of the audit	20
5.	**Auditing office accommodation**	**23**
5.1	Introduction	23
5.2	Legislation, standards and guidance	23
5.3	Collecting feedback	24
5.4	Scope and content of the audit	25

6.	**Auditing common services**	**31**
6.1	Introduction	31
6.2	Legislation, standards and guidance	31
6.3	Air conditioning	31
6.4	Ductwork and voids	34
6.5	Fire protection systems	35
6.6	Open water systems	36
6.7	Electrical installations	37
6.8	Lightning protection system	38
6.9	Emergency lighting	38
7.	**Standards and legislation**	**39**
7.1	Introduction	39
7.2	Standards	39
7.3	Legislation	39
8.	**Benefits, costs and possible problems**	**41**
8.1	Benefits	41
8.2	Costs	41
8.3	Possible problems	42
9.	**Bibliography**	**43**

Annexes

A.	Glossary of terms	A1
B.	Checklists for auditing computer accommodation	B1
C.	Checklists for auditing office accommodation	C1
D.	Model questionnaire	D1
E.	Checklists for auditing common services	E1
F.	Cleaning of computer accommodation	F1
G.	Environmental monitoring equipment	G1
H.	Model terms of reference for consultancy contracts	H1

Foreword

Welcome to the IT Infrastructure Library module on **Maintaining a Quality Environment for IT - Auditing and Cleaning.**

This module is one of a series in the Environmental Sets of the Library. In their respective areas the IT Infrastructure Library publications complement and provide more detail than the IS Guides.

The ethos behind the development of the IT Infrastructure Library is the recognition that organizations are becoming increasingly dependent on IT in order to satisfy their corporate aims and meet their business needs. This growing dependency leads to growing requirements for quality IT services. Quality means 'matched to business needs and user requirements as these evolve'.

The publications forming the major part of the Library are a series of codes of practice intended to facilitate the quality management of IT services and of the IT Infrastructure. (By IT Infrastructure, we mean an organization's computers and networks - hardware, software and computer related communications, upon which application systems and IT services are built and run). The codes of practice will assist organizations to provide quality IT services in the face of skill shortages, system complexity, rapid change, current and future user requirements, growing user expectations, etc. Details of these modules are available from CCTA Infrastructure Management Services in Gildengate House.

Supporting the IT Infrastructure is the Environmental Infrastructure. It is recognized that environmental issues, from building specification to the practicalities of cable distribution, lighting, noise, power, etc, are less well understood in IT service organizations than the IT and its infrastructure. However these issues can be just as important in delivering a quality IT service.

The Environmental Sets of modules provide guidance on addressing environmental issues. Their aim is to assist the implementation and management of an environmental infrastructure to support the needs of an organization's IT services.

IT Infrastructure Library
Maintaining a Quality Environment for IT - Auditing and Cleaning

Each module commences with a **Management summary** aimed at senior managers (Directors of IT and above, typically down to Civil Service Grade 5), senior IT staff and, in some cases, users or office managers (typically Civil Service Grades 5 to 7). The target readership for the main text is variable and identified in the **Introduction** section of each module. Wherever possible technical detail is confined to annexes.

If you have any comments on this or other modules, do please let us know. A **Comments sheet** is provided with every module. Alternatively you may wish to contact us directly using the reference points given in **Further information**.

Section 1
Management summary

1. Management summary

Background to the module

A recent survey of IT installations in central government showed problems with the environment and associated common support services such as heating, ventilation, air-conditioning and power, are one of the main contributors to IT failures. Organizations rely more and more on IT services and it is because of this increasingly high level of dependence that the quality of the environment is so important.

The quality of the working environment for IT depends on two elements:

* support for IT equipment (ie an environment that ensures the integrity, reliability and security of IT and data)

* support for IT users (ie a working environment that allows staff to work comfortably and efficiently).

Other modules in the IT Infrastructure Library series, specifically **Accommodation Specification** and **Managing a Quality Working Environment for IT Users**, deal with establishing a quality working environment for IT. This module provides guidance on how to maintain that quality working environment.

Content of the module

This module describes how to carry out audits of the environment both in dedicated computer accommodation and in offices in which a significant number of the people work with display screen equipment. The term **audit** is defined as 'a series of checks to ensure that standards for the indoor environment are maintained'. These audits are treated separately because different criteria are used. In computer accommodation, the criterion for a quality environment is how well the computer equipment is served. In offices, the criteria are human health and comfort. This module also looks at auditing common support services, at the equipment and systems which control the environment and service computer accommodation and offices.

One of the main factors that affects the operation and reliability of computers is dust. Although air-conditioning systems are important in controlling airborne dust concentrations, there must also be controls on dust and dirt coming in from outside. In Annex F guidance is given on developing suitable cleaning policies and specifications and the quality assurance checks that need to be integrated into the management of the cleaning process.

Benefits

The main benefits of introducing periodic audits of the environment for IT are that:

* compliance with health and safety legislation will be checked

* environmental conditions should be more reliable, resulting in fewer IT system breakdowns, fewer complaints about the quality of the office environment, improved productivity and reduced absenteeism, with commensurate cost savings

* maintenance standards will improve because the effectiveness of maintenance routines will be monitored.

Costs

The costs of failing to manage IT environments successfully are high:

* computer breakdowns, with, potentially, the loss of critical data

* dissatisfaction amongst employees because of a poor working environment

* the reduced reliability, efficiency and working life of building services, along with a commensurate increase in running costs

* 30 million days are lost every year in the UK due to work-related injuries and ill health (nearly 10 times the number from strikes)

* an increase of over 60% in real terms, in employers' liability insurance costs over the past decade and a doubling of claims since 1985

* sick building syndrome (SBS) which could be costing the UK economy between £300m and £650m every year in lost productivity, absenteeism and remedial works, according to the 1991 House of Commons Environment Committee. A typical organization with say 100 office-based employees, could be losing between £12,500 and £25,000 per annum because of this problem.

Such costs, whether counted in human or financial terms, can be avoided. Experience has shown that real and substantial improvements can be achieved by applying the guidance in this module.

Section 1
Management summary

Management commitment   A positive management culture needs to be developed in which environmental, and health and safety objectives are widely seen as contributing to other business goals.

Cost effective management of the IT environment needs to be carried out systematically through regular performance reviews, based on data from monitoring activities, and from independent audits, and by implementing a comprehensive cleaning and maintenance policy.

The types of auditing activity outlined in this module form the basis for self-regulation and for complying with the **Health and Safety at Work etc. Act** and other legislation. This legislation requires the identification of a Responsible Person for risk assessment. This person should be at a high level in the organization, who has a mandate to approve spending on remedial works and who has control over everyone involved in the operation and maintenance of the building, IT and common support services.

The IT Infrastructure Library
Maintaining a Quality Environment for IT - Auditing and Cleaning

2. Introduction

2.1 Purpose of module

The purpose of this module is to provide guidance on the environmental auditing of:

* computer accommodation
* office accommodation containing computer equipment including terminals and personal computers (PCs)
* common support services, such as heating, ventilation air-conditioning, water and electrical distribution and fire protection.

The information is equally applicable to sites housing all forms of electronic equipment, in particular telecommunications equipment, PABXs and tandem exchanges.

Guidance is also given on cleaning computer accommodation and office-based workstations.

This module identifies those tasks which can be carried out in-house and those that will require specialist consultants.

2.2 Target readership

This module is aimed at managers of computer accommodation and those with responsibility for the operation and maintenance of offices with a medium to high density of display terminal equipment including PCs.

2.3 Scope

Computing and display screen equipment can be sensitive to environmental conditions and maintenance standards. In turn, the presence of equipment has a major influence on the environmental conditions in which people work. The way in which this module deals with these issues is outlined below.

Audit design and management - Section 3

Firstly the module provides protocols for a formal approach to the design and management of an audit. The protocols assess compliance with:

* health and safety legislation
* fire protection legislation

The IT Infrastructure Library
Maintaining a Quality Environment for IT - Auditing and Cleaning

* design practice, as specified in other IT Infrastructure Library modules
* CCTA Model Agreements.

Auditing computer accommodation - Section 4, Annex B

This section looks at auditing computer accommodation, that is rooms which house mainframe computers and which are visited for maintenance and operational activities. It provides guidance on the parameters that need to be monitored on a regular or continuous basis, and which can be measured as part of a 'snap-shot' audit.

Auditing office accommodation - Section 5, Annexes C and D

This section deals with auditing office accommodation, that is offices where a significant proportion of people work with display screen equipment. As in Section 4, guidance is given on identifying the parameters for measurement and monitoring. The focus in this section however is on issues which effect people rather than equipment, on the effects of sedentary occupations and the long-term use of display screen equipment. In Annex D there is an example of a questionnaire which can be used for carrying out surveys.

Auditing common services - Section 6, Annex E

This section deals with auditing and inspecting the plant, equipment and distribution systems which serve computer and office accommodation. Along with Annex E it provides a summary of specific requirements for assessing compliance with health and safety legislation covering:

* fire protection
* electricity at work
* emergency lighting
* prevention or control of legionellosis.

Guidance is also given on inspecting air-conditioning equipment, ductwork and voids for identifying possible pollution sources.

Standards and legislation

This section provides a review of relevant standards and legislation.

Benefits, costs and possible problems

This section details the benefits, costs and possible problems which might result from introducing activities described in this module.

Annex F

This annex provides guidance on cleaning computer accommodation.

Annex G

This annex provides a checklist to help select equipment for monitoring aspects of the environment.

Annex H

This annex provides a checklist to help with drawing up terms of reference for the selection of external consultants.

Section 2
Introduction

2.4 Related guidance

This module is one of a series issued as part of the IT Infrastructure Library. Although the module can be read in isolation, it should be used in conjunction with other IT Infrastructure Library modules.

The following modules are of direct relevance to a quality environment and the reader is referred to them for additional information on specific topics.

Accommodation Specification provides guidance on the preparation and content of an Accommodation Design Brief for a computer centre.

Computer Operations Management gives guidance on how to plan and manage the operation of mainframe computers and related equipment.

Environmental Standards for Equipment Accommodation describes the environmental standards that were developed in conjunction with PSA and the computer manufacturer's trade association. The standards have been incorporated into the CCTA Model Agreements referred to in this module.

Human Factors in the Office Environment gives guidance on a variety of issues which affect staff in the office environment, including IT users. It covers ergonomics, strategic considerations and aspects of job design, cabling and power, health, training, environmental quality and effective use of IT.

Management of Acoustic Noise provides guidance on the identification of sources of noise and measures that can be taken to reduce such noise.

Managing a Quality Working Environment for IT Users gives guidance on four key areas associated with the quality of working environment necessary for working with IT: vision, concentration, posture and workspace.

Management of Electrical Interference describes the detrimental effects of electrical interference on IT equipment, and the protective and preventive measures that can be applied.

Office Design and Planning provides guidance on the design, planning and furnishing of an office to support IT users and to use space effectively.

Secure Power Supplies describes the techniques and equipment available to improve the quality of the electrical power supply.

2.5 Referenced documents

Documents referenced during the writing of this module are listed in the Section 9, Bibliography.

2.6 Definitions

Terms and acronyms used in this module are listed in Annex A, Glossary of terms.

2.7 Responsibilities

Health and Safety legislation requires that a Responsible Person be identified to act as a focal point for the management of health and safety matters. The Responsible Person would normally be a senior management position with a mandate for spending resources on remedial works. This person should have control over everyone involved in the operation and management of the building, IT and services. Certain responsibilities will probably need to be delegated, but the lines of responsibility and reporting procedures must be clear.

The principle of identifying a Responsible Person should also apply to auditing computer accommodation and office accommodation. For auditing computer accommodation, the Responsible Person would normally be the accommodation manager. For auditing office accommodation, the Responsible Person would normally be someone at a very senior level, with operational and managerial responsibilities for the office concerned. Although some or all of the tasks associated with the audit may need to be delegated, it is important that a quality control procedure exists and those carrying out the audit are not the same people who operate or maintain the services.

2.8 Relationships

Figure 1, overleaf, gives the main aspects of the work environment which can be measured or inspected and indicates how important auditing each aspect is:

* for the audits described in this module

* for complying with current legislation.

If a particular aspect is rated 1 ('essential'), it should be audited even if no-one has expressed concern about it. In the context of legislation an 'essential' check is one which is required to comply with a regulation.

Section 2
Introduction

For example, it is essential to check air distribution as part of an office accommodation audit. It is optional but still desirable, to check air distribution as part of the computer accommodation audit, or to comply with the Display Screen Equipment (DSE) Regulations.

Information about many of these items can be collected using a questionnaire, which forms part of the office accommodation audit. An example is given in Annex D.

The IT Infrastructure Library
Maintaining a Quality Environment for IT - Auditing and Cleaning

Aspects of the work environment	Auditing computer accom.	Auditing office accom.	Auditing common services	Display Screen Equip. Regs	Workplace Regulations	Other legislation
Air temperature	1	1	-	1	1	A
Radiant temperature	3	2	-	3	3	-
Humidity	1	1	-	1	1	-
Air velocity	3	2	-	3	3	-
Air distribution	3	1	-	3	3	-
Outdoor air supply	-	1	-	-	3	-
Airborne dust	1	3	-	-	-	B
Airborne microbes	-	3	-	-	-	B
Carbon dioxide	-	1	-	-	1	B
Carbon monoxide	-	3	-	-	3	B
Volatile organic compounds	-	3	-	-	3	B
Other gases or vapours	-	3	-	-	3	B
Lighting	2	1	-	1	1	-
Glare or reflections	2	1	-	1	1	-
Display screen image	-	1	-	1	-	-
Noise	3	1	1	1	1	C
Keyboard design	-	-	-	1	-	-
Work surface	-	2	-	1	-	-
Work chair	-	2	-	1	1	-
Task design	-	-	-	1	-	-
Human computer interaction	-	-	-	1	-	-
Space	-	-	-	1	1	-
Electromagnetic radiation	-	1	-	1	-	-
Air handling unit	-	-	1	-	-	-
Filter checks	-	-	1	-	-	-
Duct internals	-	-	1	-	-	-
Maintenance systems	-	-	1	-	1	-
Documentation	1	1	1	1	1	all
Legionellosis	-	-	1	-	3	D
Electrical safety	-	-	1	-	1	E, F
Fire safety	-	-	1	-	-	G, E
Escalators	-	-	-	-	1	E
Sanitary facilities	-	-	-	-	1	D, H
Washing facilities	-	-	-	-	1	D, H
Drinking water	-	-	-	-	1	H, I

Figure 1: Relationships between aspects of the work environment and the monitoring requirements of audit and legislation

Section 2
Introduction

Key for figure 1, opposite:

1 = essential
2 = useful
3 = optional
A = Statutory Instrument No. 1013
B = Control of Substances Hazardous to Health Regulations 1988
C = Noise at Work Regulations
D = Approved Code of Practice: Prevention or Control of Legionellosis (including legionnaires' disease) 1991
E = Electricity at Work Regulations 1989
F = Provision of and Use of Work Equipment Regulations 1992
G = Fire Precautions Act 1971
H = The Water Supply Byelaws
I = The Water Supply (Water Quality) Regulations 1989

The IT Infrastructure Library
Maintaining a Quality Environment for IT - Auditing and Cleaning

Section 3
Audit design and management

3. Audit design and management

3.1 Introduction

The term **audit**, as used in this module, is defined as 'a series of checks to ensure that standards for the indoor environment are maintained'. This section outlines a formal approach to the design and management of such an audit.

Sections 4, 5 and 6 of this module provide specific information on the scope and conduct of an audit relating to computer accommodation, office accommodation and common support services respectively.

The main phases in an audit are shown in Figure 2.

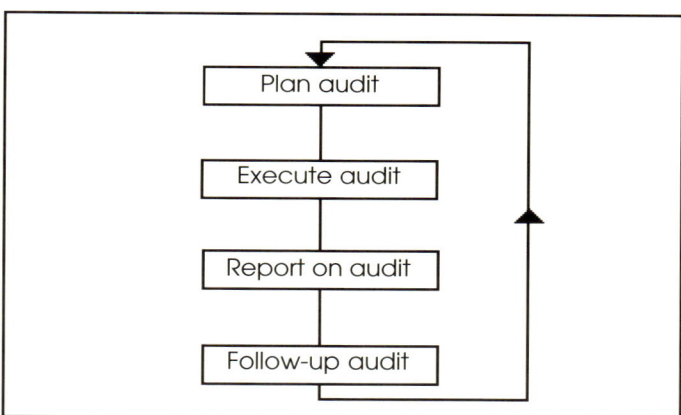

Figure 2: The audit cycle

3.2 Preparing for the first audit

The first audit requires extensive preparation. Subsequent audits are more easily prepared, since they are normally based on work done for the first audit. Preparation for an audit consists of:

* initiating an audit plan and identifying the purpose and scope of the audit
* assembling the audit team
* identifying the (performance) standards to be used (assembling the reference base)
* preparing audit checklists
* completing the audit plan.

3.2.1 Identifying the purpose and scope of the audit

The purpose of the audit should be to pinpoint any weaknesses in the design, maintenance or operation of the accommodation and common support services This should be achieved with the minimum of disruption at the site and the optimum use of audit resources.

The scope of the audit should include the functions or areas to be examined during the audit. Later sections of this module provide guidance on the range of subjects that should be included in the scope of audits for:

* computer accommodation (see Section 4.3)
* office accommodation (see Section 5.4)
* common support services (see Section 6).

The scope of an audit has a great deal of effect on its duration. A realistic scope should allow the audit to be completed in three to four days for a medium sized site.

3.2.2 Assembling the audit team

The Responsible Person (see Section 2.7) should select an audit team, which will be appropriate for the kind of audit needed. Depending on the requirements of the audit, initial work can either be carried out in house or given to specialist consultants. If outside consultants are used, terms of reference will need to be drafted (see Annex H).

Auditors should become familiar with any statutory requirements and have enough technical knowledge to take a strategic view of the auditing processes. A background in building services would be very useful.

3.2.3 Identifying performance standards to be used

Performance standards have many levels. All of these should be identified and listed in a reference base. These standards may come from the organization's policy and procedures manual or from contractual specifications, like the **Environmental Standards for Equipment Accommodation** developed by CCTA. Performance standards need to be clear and precise.

Section 3
Audit design and management

Without performance standards there can be no meaningful measurement and without measurement, audits become guesswork and not merely fact.

3.2.4 Preparing the audit checklists

Audit checklists are 'aides memoire' to guide the auditors through the functions or areas that need to be examined and to identify the parameters that need to be measured. They are a means of ensuring consistency and completeness in successive audits and provide a valuable basis for future comparison.

Key objectives of each checklist are:

* to list all aspects of each function or area which are to be audited
* to direct auditors towards analysing the results of the information they receive
* to suggest action arising from the audit.

Examples of checklists for auditing computer accommodation, office accommodation and common services can be found in Annexes B, C and E.

3.2.5 Completing the audit plan

The final stage of preparing for the audit is the completion of the audit plan which should detail:

* the audit scope and objectives
* the reference base
* the audit team
* the functions or areas to be audited, the auditees responsible, and the auditors assigned
* the date and duration of the audit
* the schedule of audit activity
* confidentiality requirements
* responsibility assigned for writing and checking the audit report
* those who will receive the audit report.

As preparation for the audit gets under way, a good deal of liaison with the auditee will be needed to fill in the details of the audit plan - for example, to identify staff responsibilities. Everyone involved will need to be aware:

* that an audit programme is under way
* of what the aims and objectives of the audit programme are
* of what is expected of them.

Generally the audit plan should be shown to the auditees so that they can arrange for interviews, the examination of relevant documents and access to plant equipment, service voids and so on. Although the actual timing of the audit should, ideally, be kept from operating and maintenance staff, they will need to be present during the audit.

Ideally the audit should be timed to coincide with the worst prevailing conditions. However this may be at different times for different parameters. For example, outdoor air pollution may be at its worst in winter but over-heating may be a problem in mid-summer. Either an optimum time will need to be chosen or a series of sub-audits carried out at different times of the year.

3.3 Executing the audit

The operational phase of the audit will be based on the requirements detailed in the audit checklists which will include tests of conformance. The aim is to assess whether products and services meet the required performance standard as detailed in the reference base.

Specific non-conformances, along with supporting evidence, should be recorded in detail.

3.4 Interpretation and follow-up action

3.4.1 Audit report

A formal written report on the audit should be prepared. The audit report should include the following information:

* audit title and other identifying information
* background information such as audit purpose, scope, dates, audit team members, and procedures used

Section 3
Audit design and management

* a brief description of the functions or areas audited
* an executive summary of any findings (of non-conformance) or observations and how they affect the organization
* specific findings (of non-conformance) or observations as attachments (see Sections 3.4.2 and 3.4.3).
* the audit report distribution list.

3.4.2 In-house reports

The in-house report should be based on the checklists in Annexes B, C and E and indicate where specialist advice has been sought, cross-referencing to the consultant's report as necessary. It should indicate which recommendations have been accepted and provide a programme for remedial works with costings and priorities.

3.4.3 Specialist consultants' reports

The consultants' terms of reference (see Annex H) should stipulate that they provide a full interpretation of their results and enough detail on remedial action to enable a designer or installer to be appointed without further surveys being needed. The consultants should be asked to provide budget costings for remedial work, along with an indication of urgency.

3.4.4 Follow-up action

The audit report should be passed to the manager of the affected area with a request for remedial action as applicable. If the report includes any non-conformances, a response detailing a course of action should be requested within a reasonable period, for example, within thirty days. This response should be evaluated to verify that:

* the cause of the problem has been identified and remedial action taken
* actions to prevent recurrence have been identified
* these actions have been, or will be, taken in a timely manner.

Additional copies of the audit report should be passed to other interested parties, for example to the Responsible Person identified to act as a focal point for the management of health and safety matters (see Section 2.7).

3.5 Preparation for second and subsequent audits

Further audits will be triggered by the following events:

* remedial works, in order to check their effectiveness
* major changes to the computer installation, its accommodation or associated services
* concerns arising from reported problems.

Should none of these events occur then auditing should be carried out at an interval which would normally be between six monthly and biennially depending on the following factors:

* the age and condition of the support plant
* the competence of the maintenance staff
* likely disruption caused by the audit
* likely cost of the audit.

Preparation for second and subsequent audits is similar but less extensive than the first. The differences are that:

* there is a previous audit report to act as the starting point for the current audit
* the existing audit checklists may need to be reviewed, and revised, to reflect any changes since the last audit.

The selection of environmental aspects to be audited may be based on a combination of criteria including:

* areas of concern from last audit
* areas that are critical to environmental conditions within the accommodation
* customer feedback.

Section 4
Auditing computer accommodation

4. Auditing computer accommodation

4.1 Introduction

This section deals with how to carry out an audit of computer accommodation as part of a preventive operating and maintenance programme. Annex B provides a checklist to help with the audit and to identify which aspects will require specialist knowledge from external consultants. Annex H provides terms of reference which might be used for the appointment of consultants.

The aim of the audit is to identify whether there are any support services or environmental conditions which do not meet legislative requirements, organizational or contractual standards, or codes of best practice. It should then propose a strategy for dealing with any problems which have been identified.

Refer to Section 6 for an inspection procedure for services, plant and equipment.

4.2 Legislation, standards and guidance

Environmental conditions and control in government computer accommodation are specified in the CCTA Model Agreements. Background guidance is given in the IT Infrastructure Library module **Environmental Standards for Equipment Accommodation**. For further information see also Section 7.

Health and safety of staff, including maintenance staff, in computer accommodation is covered by the **Health and Safety at Work etc. Act 1974**. Section 4 deals with the requirements under this act for keyboard operators.

Figure 1 shows the relationship between an audit of computer accommodation and current health and safety legislation. Figure 1 can be found on pages 10 and 11 in section 2.

4.3 Scope and conduct of the audit

4.3.1 Thermal environment and humidity

Ongoing monitoring

Temperature and humidity should be monitored continuously with a recording instrument. The main objectives of monitoring temperature and humidity are to:

* assess whether conditions drift outside specified limits over time

* to enable remedial action to be taken if necessary.

Recording instruments should be set up where they can monitor the environmental conditions experienced by the most critical equipment, but not where they will be in the way of normal operations or damaged. Avoid places which experience high radiant heat transfer (e.g. near windows or equipment), draughts, or moisture gain.

Objective

The main objectives of the thermal environment and humidity audit are to check that the monitoring has been carried out:

* satisfactorily

* in suitable places

* with recording equipment which is within acceptable tolerances.

Method

The audit should examine the records of temperature and humidity which have been kept since the previous audit or over the previous twelve months, whichever is the shorter period. Deviations from the range recommended in the desired specification (see Section 3.2.3) should be identified. If these deviations cause concern it will be necessary to investigate why they are happening. A checklist for this investigation is given in Annex B.

4.3.2 Air quality

Objective

The objective of the air quality audit is to ensure that no indoor pollutant exceeds the level at which computer equipment can operate reliably and satisfactorily.

Dust is the main air pollutant. This can damage equipment and corrupt magnetic media.

Section 4
Auditing computer accommodation

High concentrations of acidic pollutants such as oxides of nitrogen and sulphur may also damage hardware. However such high concentrations are rarely found in ambient air.

Method

There are a number of signs which may indicate dust problems. If some of these are found but are not conclusive, then airborne dust concentrations should be sampled and the source of dust identified and suitable remedial action taken (see Annex B).

If a dust problem is obvious then it may be possible to identify remedial action without having to take any measurements. However measurement of particle counts would normally form part of an audit to determine any deviation from specified levels and provide a basis for ongoing comparisons.

The main potential sources of dust in a computer room are the printers, particularly the continuously-fed type, which give off paper dust, but most printers will also give off some ribbon dust or toner powder. Concrete dust from exposed or unsealed floor or ceiling slabs may be a problem. Any accumulated surface dust may be disturbed by people or air currents. Normally these sources of potential dust problems can be found by inspection.

A common way for dust to get into computer accommodation is via the air handling system, either because the filter installation allows airborne dust to bypass the media, filters are not of the correct type, or they have not been changed at suitable intervals. Section 6 provides more information on this subject.

4.3.3 Lighting and seeing conditions

Objective

The objective of the lighting and seeing conditions audit is to ensure that the lighting conditions are suitable for people to move around in the computer room and to maintain the computer equipment.

The most critical requirements are for enough light to maintain computer equipment and for safe circulation and access when the space is occupied by people. For lighting places where people are working at display terminals for prolonged periods (see Section 5.4.4). Guidance on the lighting requirements of computer accommodation is given in the IT Infrastructure Library module **Accommodation Specification**.

Method

The audit should identify the places where close work is required and whether the working plane is vertical, horizontal or both. It should measure the illuminance accordingly.

4.3.4 Noise

Noise levels for people in computer rooms will not usually be the subject of an audit. If an increase in the noise generated by the air conditioning unit or computers has been reported or is noticed during an audit, this may indicate that something is wrong and may warrant further investigation by a specialist.

4.3.5 Electric and magnetic fields

Objective

The objective of the electric and magnetic fields audit is to identify any factors which indicate excessive electric and magnetic interference.

A mainframe computer should be in an acceptable electromagnetic environment with an appropriate supply voltage waveform.

Method

Electrical equipment must not produce electric and magnetic fields above certain intensities and has to function satisfactorily in extraneous fields up to a certain intensity. If a known source of electric and magnetic interference (eg. a (nearby) radar scanner) has made its appearance since the computer system was commissioned, and the equipment's reliability has decreased coincidentally with this, then field strength measurements may be required; expert advice should be sought.

Refer also to the IT Infrastructure Library module **Management of Electrical Interference**.

5. Auditing office accommodation

5.1 Introduction

This section deals with how to carry out audits of office accommodation in which a significant proportion of people are working at display screen equipment. The audit and associated monitoring programme, form part of a preventive strategy which aims to provide a supportive environment for both people and equipment. This should lead to fewer equipment breakdowns, fewer complaints about the office environment, improved productivity and reduced absenteeism.

The core diagnostic tool for the audit is an environmental conditions questionnaire, from which important data can be gleaned about people's perceptions, any reported symptoms and any work-related problems. Annex D provides a model questionnaire which can be adapted for specific needs.

Annex C provides a checklist for the audit, and for analysing the results from the questionnaire. This checklist also shows where remedial action might be recommended without further investigation.

These checks do not replace an assessment of compliance with the **Health and Safety (Display Screen Equipment) Regulations 1992** or the **Workplace (Health, Safety and Welfare) Regulations 1992**. Proof of compliance with these Regulations is an essential ingredient of the checks (see also the OHS/CCTA Checklist for the Assessment and Analysis of Visual Display Screen Equipment Workstations).

5.2 Legislation, standards and guidance

Although the environmental standards for a range of situations is specified in the CCTA Model Agreements these do not cover all comfort criteria. Guidance published by the Chartered Institution of Building Services Engineers (CIBSE) in their **Environmental criteria for design** and various lighting publications provides criteria for office applications. **CIBSE's Lighting Guide LG3 : 1989 Areas for visual display terminals** and **Applications Manual AM7 : 1992 Information technology and buildings** provide specific guidance on the design of support services for offices containing computer equipment.

The Health and Safety (Display Screen Equipment) Regulations 1992 address a wide range of issues relating to health and safety of people using workstations. Those pertaining to the indoor environment are relevant to this module.

The Workplace (Health, Safety and Welfare) Regulations provide broad brush requirements covering a wide variety of factors including:

- ventilation
- temperature
- noise
- lighting
- sanitary facilities
- drinking water
- building fabric.

The regulations are mostly non-specific, typically requiring a given factor to be 'suitable and sufficient'.

Other relevant legislation includes the following:

- **Offices Shops and Railway Premises Act**
- **Noise at Work Regulations**.

Figure 1, pages 10 & 11, shows the relationship between audit requirements and current health and safety legislation.

5.3 Collecting feedback

People are usually good judges of their own working environments. A questionnaire should be used to gather up-to-date information on people's perceptions, any reported symptoms or other factors which may generate work-related problems. Annex D gives a model questionnaire which can be adapted to specific needs.

The questionnaire may help to target what to look at by identifying the high incidence of specific problems and clusters of complaints and symptoms. This information will be used to design the physical survey programme, and to brief specialist consultants.

The questionnaire covers:

- * the environment:
    - space
    - light
    - glare
    - heat
    - humidity
    - air quality
    - air movement
    - noise
- * symptoms experienced at work, but which largely disappear when away from the workplace
- * other factors which may influence the reporting of perceptions and symptoms, such as job type, gender etc.

As well as the questionnaire the following sources of information should also be available to the auditor:

- * a logbook recording complaints about the working environment (see Annex F)
- * reports from the health and safety committee
- * available reports on work related absenteeism.

5.4 Scope and content of the audit

5.4.1 Thermal environment and air movement

Ongoing monitoring

Room temperature should ideally be continuously monitored with either portable or fixed thermometers or a recording instrument. Where there is humidity control or concern about extremes of humidity a hygrometer should also be used. These are frequently combined with thermometers. These instruments should be recalibrated regularly, according to type and experience.

The IT Infrastructure Library
Maintaining a Quality Environment for IT - Auditing and Cleaning

Recording instruments should be set up in positions which are representative of the environment experienced by the occupants, but not where they are in the way or likely to be damaged. Sensing heads should be at approximately 1.1 m from the floor. Avoid places which experience high radiant heat transfer (e.g. near windows or equipment), draughts, or moisture gain.

Objective

The objective of the thermal environment and air movement audit is to confirm that temperature and relative humidity are within specified limits.

Method

The auditor should examine records of temperature and humidity that have been kept since the previous audit or over the last 12 months, whichever is the shorter period. The accuracy of the recording equipment should be checked against calibrated equipment. If causes for concern are identified from the monitoring records, or from an analysis of the questionnaire survey, then a detailed thermal environment survey should be carried out. If air movement also appears to be a problem then it will be necessary to measure room air velocities and carry out smoke tests on the supply air terminal devices (see Section 5.4.3). Similarly if problems due to people being seated close to high or low temperature surfaces are suspected then radiant temperatures should be checked.

For thermal environment surveys a number of measurement stations which represent problem areas should be identified - e.g. where there have been clusters of complaints. Instruments should be placed at or close to workstations, and measurements obtained of:

* air dry bulb temperature
* relative humidity
* mean omnidirectional velocity, if necessary (see Annex C.1)
* globe temperature, if necessary (see Annex C.1).

5.4.2 Air quality

Objective

The objective of the air quality audit is to check the quality of any air coming from either an the air-conditioning unit or from a ventilating system.

There are a number of indoor air pollutants to look for. Some of these are:

* *house dust;* this is one of the most common pollutants

Section 5
Auditing office accommodation

* *volatile organic compounds (VOCs)*; VOCs include solvent vapours such as toluene and xylene, which are used in the manufacture of

  - sealants
  - floor coverings
  - furniture
  - paints
  - correction fluids
  - cleaning agents

* *airborne fungal spores*; these can produce allergic reactions in susceptible individuals

* *mould*; mould growing in air-handling systems gives off a strong smell

* *smoking*; where smoking is allowed and where smokers and non-smokers work alongside each other, non-smokers are usually uncomfortable because of the strong smell of tobacco, even if outdoor air-supply rates exceed recommended values

* *ozone*; this is a short-lived reactive gas generated from photocopiers and laser printers

* *formaldehyde*; this is used in the manufacture of blown insulation, particle board, fabrics and wall coverings.

Outdoor pollutants may also be a problem, particularly:

* exhaust fumes
* gaseous pollutants.

Method

Accurately measuring the low concentrations of these substances normally found in office buildings requires fairly sophisticated and expensive equipment (see Annex G). In most air quality audits it will only be necessary to identify the sources of air pollutants, analyze the questionnaire for complaints about odour and carry out a ventilation survey to assess how effective the outdoor air supply is at diluting odours indoors.

5.4.3 Outdoor air supply

Objective The objective of the outdoor air supply audit is to confirm that the amount of outdoor air supplied meets the criteria for office accommodation.

Method The simplest and cheapest method for estimating outdoor air supply rate is to measure:

* the concentration of carbon dioxide in the room

* the concentration of carbon dioxide in air supplied to that room

* the emission rate of carbon dioxide into the room from the people working in it (this can be estimated at 0.005 litres/s per sedentary person).

The outdoor air supply rate per person (Q_O) is calculated from:

$$Q_O = \frac{5000}{C_R - C_S} \text{ litres per second}$$

where C_R = concentration of CO_2 in room (ppm) and C_S = concentration of CO_2 in supply air (ppm)

Recommendations for rates of outdoor air supply per person are given in the **CIBSE Guide 1986, Section B2 : Ventilation and air conditioning (requirements)**.

The effectiveness of the air distribution system can be gauged by:

* smoke tests; these may be used to show whether there is short-circuiting between the air supply and air extract systems (remember to override smoke detection and smoke-actuated sprinkler systems before starting these tests)

* comparing air distribution rates measured by the above method with the volume flow rate of outdoor air being drawn in through the fresh air inlet duct (if this is accessible for accurate measurement); if the former is significantly lower (<75%) this could indicate that short circuiting is occurring, either:

  - from the exhaust to the fresh air inlet

  - from the supply to extract openings

  - by leakage between supply and extract ducts.

Section 5
Auditing office accommodation

5.4.4 Lighting and seeing conditions

Objective

The objective of the lighting and seeing conditions audit is to assess what contribution the office lighting and the visual environment may be making to the symptoms of tired and aching eyes, headaches and fatigue, which are associated with long periods of working at visual display systems.

The results of the questionnaire should indicate whether there are significant problems, particularly if there is a high incidence of complaints about lighting conditions and screen reflections, combined with eye symptoms and headaches.

There is significant overlap between this audit and the workstation assessment required to check conformity with the **Health and Safety (Display Screen Equipment) Regulations 1992**.

Method

Checks should be made to examine potential causes of eye strain, such as:

* reflections in the screen
* poor definition and stability of screen images
* poor illumination
* poor contrast
* poor positioning of documents.

The design and positioning of the screen and keyboard should also be reviewed. Light levels should be measured at places which correspond to normal staff work stations.

5.4.5 Noise

Objective

The objective of the noise audit is to confirm that noise levels in the office areas fall within generally recommended guidelines.

If there are a significant number of complaints about noise in the questionnaires it will be necessary to identify where the noise comes from and to investigate whether noise levels can be reduced. The main sources of noise may be outdoors, or from the building services, office machinery or people. Noise levels may vary depending on the distances between the sources of noise and where people work.

Method

An initial check should identify the most significant sources of noise, i.e. those to which people are most sensitive.

Sound pressure level (SPL) or noise rating (NR) measurements should be taken at various points which correspond to normal staff work stations and in what seem to be the noisiest places.

Refer to the **CIBSE Guide 1986, Section A1: Environmental Criteria for Design** for recommended levels of noise for various applications. If recommended noise criteria are exceeded then a specialist survey may be required in order to identify what can be done.

If there appears to be too much noise or vibration from external sources a check should be made to find out whether it is temporary or not. If noise from neighbouring sources outdoors is causing a nuisance the local environmental health officer should be consulted. If unavoidable traffic noise is the problem, advice should be sought on how to seal the routes it takes into the building, bearing in mind that a double-glazed, sealed building would require mechanical ventilation.

If increasing noise levels from machinery are identified in successive audits then this may indicate motor wear or a developing fault. The problem should be referred to the maintenance section (or contractors).

Refer also the IT Infrastructure Library module **Management of Acoustic Noise**.

5.4.6 Electric and magnetic fields

Objective

The objective of the electric and magnetic fields audit is to identify any factors which indicate excessive electric and magnetic interference.

Method

Electrical equipment must not produce electric and magnetic fields above certain intensities and it has to function satisfactorily in extraneous fields up to a certain intensity. If a known source of electric and magnetic interference (eg. a (nearby) radar scanner) has made its appearance since the computer equipment was commissioned, and the equipment's reliability has decreased coincidentally with this, expert advice should be sought.

The magnetic field associated with power cables can affect display screen equipment causing a small movement of characters on the screen. If such interference is present then power frequency field strengths should be measured and compared with recommended levels.

Refer also to the IT Infrastructure Library module **Management of Electrical Interference** for guidance on permitted levels.

Section 6
Auditing common services

6. Auditing common services

6.1 Introduction

This section deals with auditing the support services for computer accommodation or offices in which computers are located. This section should be used in conjunction with the auditing procedures for the environments described in Sections 4 and 5 respectively. Refer to Annex E for checklists to help implementing these audits. Guidance is also given on which tasks are likely to require specialist expertise.

6.2 Legislation, standards and guidance

The main legislative requirements and supporting guidance are described under each of the following sections. Electrical equipment and water systems which create an inhalable aerosol are covered by health and safety legislation. Electrical distribution systems are covered by the **IEE Wiring Regulations (BS 7671)**. Fire precautions and emergency lighting are assessed under fire legislation. See also Section 7 - Standards and legislation.

6.3 Air conditioning

Air conditioning covers ways of heating, cooling and ventilating computer accommodation or offices. Most air-conditioning plants also provide some dehumidification and some will humidify during cold spells. There are many different ways of providing air conditioning, some of which provide tighter control over room conditions than others. It is beyond the scope of this publication to provide detailed guidance on methods of air conditioning. Further information can be found in the **CIBSE Guide 1986, Section B3 : Air conditioning systems, equipment and control** and the **CIBSE IT Applications Manual** (see also Section 9 - Bibliography).

The main criterion for the design and operation of air conditioning systems is that they must be able to maintain internal conditions within specified limits.

Problems with air conditioning will usually be identified during monitoring or auditing of the indoor environment. However, to keep air-conditioning running in a relatively trouble-free way in the long term, three routines should be used:

The IT Infrastructure Library
Maintaining a Quality Environment for IT - Auditing and Cleaning

1. regular auditing
2. preventive maintenance
3. monitoring and remedial action.

Check the condition of the air-conditioning equipment just before it is due for internal cleaning, and the filters changed or cleaned, to see whether the yearly maintenance check is actually necessary.

6.3.1 Filter installation

Objective

The objective of an audit of a filter installation is to ensure that filters:

* are suitable
* are being maintained satisfactorily
* are not being by-passed by dust.

There are many different types of filter. Some may be no more than a screen, capable of removing large particles only. These may be found at the inlet to many types of fan coil unit, and are usually washable. At the other end of the scale are high efficiency particulate air (hepa) filters, which can remove most particles down to sub-micron size. These are typically found in the air supply to clean rooms and, provided they are protected by upstream filters, can last for several years before replacement.

Method

During an audit, maintenance records should be inspected:

* to ascertain the intervals at which filters are changed or washed
* to compare these intervals with what would be expected for the type of filter and the prevailing air quality.

This interval will normally be determined from experience. As an approximate guide most fibre filters would not last much longer than 6 weeks in a large town or city, whereas bag-type filters which are protected from larger particles by a pre-filter installation could last for up to a year. The filter installation should be inspected for leakage paths around filters and the downstream face of each filter should be inspected for signs of dust penetration. It is useful to compare its colour and condition with a new one.

Section 6
Auditing common services

Most filter installations are equipped with a differential manometer which is sometimes used to judge when a filter should be changed or washed. An audit should find out whether maintenance staff use this device and its calibration should be checked.

6.3.2 Air handling plant and equipment

Objective

The objective of the air handling plant and equipment audit is to check that the internal condition of the air handling plant is satisfactory and it contains no pollution source.

In the context of this module 'air handling plant' is defined as any device which contains a fan and heat exchangers, ranging from fan coil units to central plant equipment.

These devices will normally contain finned heat exchangers, which can trap any large particles which find their way past the filters. Where dehumidifying coils are fitted, condensate runs down the fins and should be carried away via a condensate tray and drainage systems, as any dirt which collects in this tray could act as a site for microbiological growth. Spray humidifiers and spray coils are a hazard, particularly if water remains standing in the pond during warm periods. Spray humidification is rarely found nowadays, and has mostly been superseded by steam injection, which provides a sterile source of moisture. However, if steam humidifiers are installed with obstructions, such as bends, branches and sound attenuators, within 1.5m downstream a number of problems can result:

* condensation
* accumulation of scale
* rust
* microbiological growth.

Method

An audit should include a physical inspection of the internal condition of the air handling plant (see Annex E.1.1).

6.3.3 Controls

Objective

The objective of the controls audit is to check that all controls are functioning as intended and that accuracy of control is to the required specification.

The IT Infrastructure Library
Maintaining a Quality Environment for IT - Auditing and Cleaning

Air conditioning plant and equipment cannot function properly or efficiently if control sensors are out of calibration. All sensors, whether in ducts, rooms or pipes will require regular (condition) checks, and the maintenance schedule should allow for periodic cleaning of all sensors.

Method

An audit should check maintenance and calibration records and check the accuracy of some of the more critical sensors.

6.4 Ductwork and voids

Objective

The objective of the ductwork and voids audit is to check the internal surfaces of the air distribution systems for signs of soiling, rusting and leaks.

Most existing ductwork systems have not been designed with access in mind, either for inspection or for cleaning. In fact, if there has always been a high standard of filtration upstream of a ducted air distribution system the ductwork should be clean internally. However there should be concern about the internal condition of the ductwork if any of the following indicators are noticed:

* maintenance records indicate lapses in filter replacement or washing

* the internal condition of the air handling plant is poor

* there are signs of severe dust penetration and/or filters being by-passed by dust

* information from cleaners reveals that internal surfaces of rooms become dirty more rapidly than would be expected, when internal sources of dust are accounted for

* the ductwork system has been in place for many years without attention.

Method

Dust will settle most easily in low velocity regions, such as floor and ceiling voids, and on rough and absorbent surfaces such as acoustic duct linings and flexible ductwork. If there are signs of deposits in the air handling plant (see Section 6.3.2) other low velocity regions, such as plenum connections to air terminal devices should be inspected and tested for levels of deposit with adhesive tape or a damp cloth. Access to the distribution ductwork may also be possible via access hatches: these should have been provided where ductwork passes through fire barriers, in order to reset fire dampers.

Section 6
Auditing common services

If normal access is impossible it may be necessary to commission a borescope survey of internal surfaces. This will involve drilling holes in the duct walls at strategic points and inserting a fibre-optic tube connected to a light-source and an eye-piece or camera.

6.5 Fire protection systems

Objective

The objective of the fire protection systems audit is to check that an assessment of risk has been carried out in compliance with Regulations and that the conditions under which the current fire certificate was issued still prevail.

Potential sources of fire in computer accommodation are:

* the computer equipment itself
* the electrical distribution system
* the air conditioning equipment.

Extinguishing systems may be either manual or automatic, employing either halon or CO_2 gas, including portable fire extinguishers at key locations.

Fire prevention procedures should have been developed in conjunction with the Local Fire Prevention Officer. Written procedures should be posted and there should be regular rehearsals of evacuation and shut-down procedures.

When the **Fire Precautions (Places of Work) Regulations** come into force, an assessment of fire risk and precautions (at the place of work) will be mandatory. The regulations are expected to pass through Parliament in 1994.

Refer also to the IT Infrastructure Library module **Fire Precautions in IT Installations**.

Method

Auditing fire protection systems includes checking:

* the building's fire protection certificate
* means of escape
* fire alarms systems
* automatic fire detection systems
* extinguishing systems.

A detailed checklist has been included in Annex E.4.

6.6 Open water systems

Objective

The objective of the open water systems audit is to ensure that assessments of risk have been carried out in compliance with legionellosis legislation.

Open water systems, such as domestic water systems and evaporative cooling towers, can produce an inhalable aerosol which may transmit legionellosis, a syndrome which includes legionnaire's disease and Pontiac fever.

With the introduction of an **Approved Code of Practice - Prevention or control of legionellosis (including legionnaire's disease)** in 1992, water has been classified as a substance which is potentially hazardous to health under the **COSHH Regulations 1988**. This means that people who have responsibility for operating these systems must carry out an assessment of risk and ensure that adequate control measures are in place.

For auditing water systems, the issues which must be considered are:

* design
* operation and maintenance
* management
* reporting and communications
* staff competence and training.

Method

The audit of a water system would check that an assessment of risk has been carried out, and, if a risk has been identified, that a full programme of preventive and control measures has been implemented and its effectiveness checked. Annex E.2 summarises the main risk factors and the elements which should be examined to check whether the assessment has been carried out properly. A full assessment should be commissioned if:

* the schedule assessment has not been carried out
* major changes which affect risk have occurred since the last assessment
* there is concern about the effectiveness of the preventive or control schedule.

Section 6
Auditing common services

6.7 Electrical installations

Objective

The objective of the electrical installation audit is to check that legislative requirements for minimising the risk of electrocution or fire from electrical equipment or distribution systems have been fulfilled.

Method

Electrical equipment should have been tested in order to comply with the requirements of the **Electricity at Work Regulations 1989**. The electrical distribution system should have a certificate of compliance with the **IEE Wiring Regulations**. If there is concern about compliance with either of these regulations then a survey should be commissioned. Annex E.3 provides a checklist of factors which should be examined to check whether an assessment has been carried out.

Part of the audit should include an assessment of the potential discomfort people may experience from electrostatic shock. If there have been complaints the resistance of the floor covering should be measured. Refer to **BS 5958 : Part 1**.

Uninterruptible power supply and standby generators

The uninterruptible power supply (UPS) should be checked by an appropriately qualified person under simulated emergency conditions. When the mains supply is switched off there should be no interruption to the computer operation. The battery voltage measured at an appropriate point in the circuit should be reduced and the starting mechanism of the standby generator and its automatic connection to the UPS checked. When the mains supply is restored the standby generator should be shut down. A check should also be made that automatic rapid switching directly to the mains is taking place by reducing the UPS output voltage accordingly.

Auditing the standby generator should include checking:

* of the generator fuel system
* the fuel tanks (for leaks)
* generator noise
* the frequency of generator tests (carried out according to a pre-defined schedule).

Refer also to IT Infrastructure Library module **Secure Power Supplies**.

6.8 Lightning protection system

Objective — The objective of a lightning protection system audit is to ensure that the building and equipment within the building are adequately protected from a lightning strike in line with current standards.

Method — Check that a lightning protection system has been installed. If it has, check documentary evidence that inspection and testing has been carried out in accordance with current standards. If this has not been done or major changes have occurred to the building since the last audit then a full test should be commissioned.

6.9 Emergency lighting

Objective — The objective of the emergency lighting audit is to ensure that there is enough light for a safe exit in the event of a power failure.

Method — The audit should ensure that the minimum standard, which requires 0.2 lux to be available within 5 seconds of a loss of power, is attained.

7. Standards and legislation

7.1 Introduction

Environmental conditions in government computer accommodation are specified in the CCTA Model Agreements. It should be noted that **BS 7083: 1989 - Accommodation and operating of computer equipment**, covers similar ground, but some of the values specified for environmental conditions are different. In most circumstances an audit should provide a check against the contractual specification.

Regulations exist which cover:

* electrical appliances
* substances hazardous to health (including legionella)
* work with display screen equipment
* health and safety management
* workplace standards
* work equipment
* protective equipment and manual handling.

The lists below indicate the areas covered by particular standards and pieces of legislation.

7.2 Standards

British Standard **BS7179: 1990, Ergonomics of design and use of Visual Display Terminals (VDTs) in offices** gives design guidance for offices where the majority of people are working with visual display terminals. It will be superseded by ISO 9241 or EN 29241.

British Standard **BS7671: 1992, IEE Wiring Regulations** provide minimum safety standards for electrical installations.

7.3 Legislation

The **Health and Safety at Work etc Act, 1974**, and its associated Regulations and Codes of Practice provide minimum legal standards to ensure that people are not put at risk during their working day.

The **European Workplace Directives, 1993**, are incorporated into the Health and Safety at Work etc Act. The emphasis is on assessment of risk and implementing a system of prevention or control.

The **Offices, Shops and Railway Premises Act, 1973**, sets out certain standards concerning minimum temperatures and ventilation rates. They are well below the standards recommended by the Chartered Institution of Building Services Engineers however. This Act is superseded by the Workplace (Health, Safety and Welfare) Regulations.

The **Workplace (Health, Safety and Welfare) Regulations, 1993**, incorporate general provisions but even the associated guidance notes associated with the Regulations do not specify values for environmental conditions or ventilation.

The **Health and Safety (Display Screen Equipment) Regulations 1993**, provide requirements for workstation design, indoor environment, human computer interaction and so on.

The **Electricity at Work Regulations, 1989**, cover the safety of electrical equipment.

The **Fire Precautions (Places of Work) Regulations** will require assessment of risk to be carried out for all places of work with more than five people working there.

Section 8
Benefits, costs and possible problems

8. Benefits, costs and possible problems

8.1 Benefits

There are a number of arguments which can be used to justify introducing a system of monitoring and periodic audits or checks on environmental conditions and support services:

* compliance with health and safety legislation will be checked

* the reliability of environmental conditions should improve resulting in fewer equipment breakdowns, fewer complaints about a poor office environment, improved productivity and reduced absenteeism, with commensurate cost savings (see Section 8.2)

* maintenance standards will improve because there will be opportunities to see the effectiveness of maintenance routines

* the questionnaire provides opportunities for consultation with staff and provides invaluable feedback on their perceptions of their working environment

* monitoring environmental conditions and carrying out regular checks on plant and equipment will show up areas where plant operates inefficiently and hence provide opportunities for energy savings.

8.2 Costs

Both monitoring and auditing involve extra expenditure which will add to the running costs of the computer accommodation. The benefits of auditing can be assessed by monitoring productivity, absenteeism and the incidence of breakdown some time before the initial audits are carried out, and periodically after that. Any improvements can be costed and compared with the cost of the audits or checks and remedial action.

The cost of auditing the accommodation and associated support services for a business with office-based employees would depend on the complexity of the services, the amount of investigative work required and the proportion of work which can be carried out in-house. For a business with, say, 100 office-based employees an external consultant might charge anything between £3,000 and £10,000 (at 1993 prices) for an audit. An external audit of typical main-frame

The IT Infrastructure Library
Maintaining a Quality Environment for IT - Auditing and Cleaning

computer accommodation and services is likely to cost upwards of £1,500. On top of this there would in-house resource costs, including staff-time, training, equipment etc, and the cost of remedial works. However, such works, being preventive rather than corrective, might be cheaper than waiting for things to go wrong.

8.3 Possible problems

Auditing can be an intrusive activity and some staff, particularly those whose work is being scrutinised, may feel threatened. To help manage this problem it is important to initiate an awareness campaign. The cooperation of maintenance staff is essential to complete the audit successfully. It is important that they recognize that the audit is an integral part of the management system for the accommodation, and cooperation with the auditors should ideally be part of the conditions of any maintenance contract.

It may not always be possible to obtain a full response to a self-administered questionnaire. For the best results it is important to explain the purpose and benefits of the survey and it should be made clear that the responses will remain confidential. Some staff may fear victimisation if they are critical in their responses.

Many organizations are unlikely to have sufficient expertise in-house to undertake the technical aspects of the audits. Specialist consultants would normally be able to offer a cost-effective and independent package to cover an audit programme.

Problems encountered by organisations attempting to carry out part or all of an audit in-house are likely to include:

* lack of training in correct procedures

* lack of specialist equipment

* demands on staff which may disrupt the audit programme

* lack of objectivity and independence which may influence the interpretation of the results

* cost penalties which may arise if an external specialist needs to be appointed when problems appear.

Section 9
Bibliography

9. Bibliography

Approved Code of Practice - Prevention or control of legionellosis (including legionnaire's disease); Health and Safety Commission 1991

BS 5958 : 1989 - Code of practice for control of undesirable static electricity, Part 1 - General considerations; British Standards Institution 1989

BS 7083 : 1989 - Recommendations for the Accommodation and operating environment of computer equipment; British Standards Institution 1989

BS 7179 : 1990 - Ergonomics of design and use of visual display terminals (VDTs) in offices; British Standards Institution 1990

CIBSE Guide - Section A1 : Environmental criteria for design; Chartered Institution of Building Services Engineers 1986

CIBSE Lighting Guide - LG3 : Areas for visual display terminals; Chartered Institution of Building Services Engineers 1989

CIBSE Applications Manual - AM7 : Information Technology and Buildings; Chartered Institution of Building Services Engineers 1992

CIBSE Technical Memorandum - TM13 : Minimising the risk of Legionnaires' disease; Chartered Institution of Building Services Engineers 1991

Control of Substances Hazardous to Health Regulations 1989

Housekeeping Guide for Accommodation Managers; Department of Environment (undated)

Electricity at Work Regulations 1989

Fire Precautions (Places of Work) Regulations (to be published)

Health and Safety at Work etc. Act 1974

Health and Safety (Display screen equipment) Regulations 1992; Health and Safety (Display screen equipment work) Guidance on Regulations; Health and Safety Executive 1992

House of Commons Environment Committee - Sixth Report: Indoor Pollution; HMSO 1991

IEE Wiring Regulations 16th Edition (BS 7671:1992)

Workplace (Health, Safety and Welfare) Regulations 1992

Annex A. Glossary of terms

Acronyms and abbreviations used in the module

AHU	Air handling unit
ACoP	Approved Code of Practice
CEN	Comité Européen de Normalisation (European Committee for Standardisation)
CENELEC	European Committee for electrical standards
C_R	Concentration in room
C_O	Concentration in outdoor air
CO_2	Carbon dioxide
COSHH	Control of Substances Hazardous to Health
EC	European Council
hepa	High efficiency particulate air
IT	Information technology
NR	Noise rating
ppm	Parts per million
Q_O	Outdoor air supply rate per person
SBS	Sick building syndrome
SPL	Sound pressure level
UPS	Uninterruptible power supply
VDT	Visual display terminal
VDU	Visual display unit
VOC	Volatile organic compound

The IT Infrastructure Library
Maintaining a Quality Environment for IT - Auditing and Cleaning

Definitions used in the module

air distribution system	A system of ductwork which distributes air throughout a building.
air handling unit	A device which treats incoming air and blows it through a system of ductwork into the building. It usually comprises filters, heat exchangers and fan.
air terminal device	A device through which air is transferred to or from an area.
audit (environmental)	A series of checks to ensure that indoor standards are maintained.
CCTA Model Agreements	CCTA contract conditions covering the whole range of information systems contracting.
condensate	A product of condensation, especially a liquid obtained by condensation of a gas or vapour.
display screen equipment	Any alphanumeric or graphic display screen, regardless of the display process involved.
dry bulb temperature	The air temperature measured by a thermometer which is protected from thermal radiation.
dry resultant temperature	The temperature recorded by a thermometer at the centre of a blackened globe 100 mm in diameter, used as a comfort index in the UK.
electric field	A field of force extending between points where there is an electric potential difference (voltage).
electromagnetic environment	The sum total of electric and magnetic fields from local electrical equipment and geomagnetic sources, and including radiation from radio and radar stations (which has both electric and magnetic components).
extract air	Air which is removed from an area.
filter installation	The filter and the frame in which it is mounted.
fresh air inlet	The outdoor air intake.
globe temperature	The temperature measured by a matt black sphere with a thermometer at its centre: approximates to dry resultant temperature.
human auditory system	The receptors and transmitters in humans which receive sound waves and relay signals to the brain.

Annex A
Glossary of terms

illuminance	The luminous flux density at a surface, i.e. the level of illumination.
litres/s	Unit of volume flow rate, where 1 litre per second = 10^{-3} cubic metres per second.
lumen	Unit of luminous flux, used in describing the quantity of light emitted by a source or received by a surface.
lux	Unit of illuminance equal to one lumen per square metre.
magnetic field	A field of force surrounding an electric current.
mean omnidirectional velocity	The air velocity at a point averaged over time.
monitoring	An ongoing survey.
open water system	A system comprising a combination of pipes, water storage devices and heat exchangers which is open to the atmosphere.
outdoor air supply rate	The volume flow of outdoor air required to meet the hygiene needs of occupants, and principally to dilute odours to an acceptable level.
plenum	Part of an air distribution system where velocities are at a low level.
radiant heat transfer	Transfer of heat from one surface to another by radiation.
relative humidity	The ratio of the amount of water present in a quantity of air to the maximum amount of moisture that the air can hold at the same temperature.
Responsible Person	The person on whom the statutory duty falls to carry out risk assessments under the **Health and Safety at Work etc. Act 1974**.
sick building syndrome	A collection of symptoms experienced by a significant proportion of occupants of a building which diminish or disappear when they leave that building.
smoke detector	A device which responds to the presence of smoke by setting off an alarm.
smoke test	A visualisation of air flow patterns using a low-toxicity source of neutral buoyancy particles.
smoke tube	A sealed tube containing a substance which generates a fine neutral buoyancy smoke when exposed to air.

The IT Infrastructure Library
Maintaining a Quality Environment for IT - Auditing and Cleaning

supply air	Air which is distributed throughout a building by an air handling plant and blown into rooms through grilles or diffusers in order to heat, cool, humidify, dehumidify and ventilate as appropriate.
survey	Investigation of a specific aspect of the indoor environment or inspection of plant and equipment.
visual display terminal	A screen display and keyboard.
volatile organic compound	A carbon-based chemical which evaporates when exposed to normal ambient conditions.
workstation	An assembly comprising display screen equipment, accessories, disk drives, telephone, modem, printer, document holder, work chair, work desk, other work surfaces and peripheral items, and the immediate work environment around the display screen equipment.

Annex B. Checklists for auditing computer accommodation

Note: The actions marked with a hash (#) may require specialist knowledge.

B.1 Thermal and humidity surveys

Audit observations

Check:

* recording instruments
    - positioning ☐
    - calibration records ☐
    - accuracy ☐
* sensor settings ☐
* surfaces for signs of moisture damage ☐
* surfaces for signs of mould growth ☐
* temperature records ☐
* humidity records ☐

Analysis of results

Complete the analysis using information from the audit observations. If all the answers are 'yes' no further action needs to be taken. If any answer is 'no' go to *Action*.

YES NO

* recording instrument accurate ☐ ☐
* surfaces free of moisture damage or mould growth ☐ ☐
* recorded value match specified values ☐ ☐
* 'snapshot' readings match specification ☐ ☐

Action

* check design of thermal systems# (see Section 6) ☐
* check performance of thermal systems# (see Section 6) ☐
* check calibration of sensors# ☐
* install monitoring instruments ☐
* recommend remedial action# ☐

B 1

The IT Infrastructure Library
Maintaining a Quality Environment for IT - Auditing and Cleaning

B.2 Air quality survey

Audit observations

Check:

* air filters
  - type# (see Section 6) ☐
  - efficiency# (see Section 6) ☐
  - maintenance records# ☐
  - catching all polluted air ☐
* annual particulate count records ☐

Analysis of results

Complete the analysis using information from the audit observations. If all the answers are 'yes', then no further action needs to be taken. If any answer is 'no', and there is conclusive evidence that dust is a problem, go to *Action*. If any answer is 'no', and there is not conclusive evidence that dust is a problem, specialist help may be required to solve the problem.

YES   NO

* air filters functioning properly ☐ ☐
* recorded particulate levels within specified levels ☐ ☐
* fault free operation ☐ ☐
* constant levels of surface dust ☐ ☐

Action

* identify source of dust
  - in room ☐
  - in supply air ducts (see Section 6) ☐
  - in plenums (see Section 6) ☐
  - in plant (see Section 6) ☐
  - outdoors (inadequate filter installation) (see Section 6) ☐

If indicators are not conclusive, an investigation by specialists may be required.

Annex B
Checklists for auditing computer accommodation

B.3 Lighting and seeing conditions survey

Audit observations   Check:

* light levels where computer maintenance is carried out ☐
* presence of glare ☐
* presence of shadowing ☐

Analysis of results   Complete the analysis using information from the audit observations. If the answer is 'yes', no further action needs to be taken. If the answer is 'no', go to *Action*.

                                  YES NO
* lighting conditions correct for tasks ☐ ☐

Action

* recommend remedial action ☐

B.4 Noise survey

Audit observations   Check:

* levels of noise ☐
* opinions of any increase in noise, from operators ☐
* opinions of any increase in noise, from auditors ☐

Analysis of results   Complete the analysis using information from the audit observations. If the answers are 'yes', no further action needs to be taken. If any answer is 'no', go to *Action*.

                                  YES NO
* noise levels within specification limits ☐ ☐
* noise levels constant ☐ ☐

Action

* re-measure noise levels# ☐
* recommend remedial action ☐

The IT Infrastructure Library
Maintaining a Quality Environment for IT - Auditing and Cleaning

B.5 Electric and magnetic fields survey

Audit observations Check:

* likely sources of interference ☐

Analysis of results Complete the analysis using information from the audit observations. If the answer is 'yes', no further action needs to be taken. If the answer is 'no', go to *Action*.

YES NO

* no unexplained operational problems ☐ ☐

Action

* arrange for field strength measurements to be undertaken by a specialist# ☐

Annex C. Checklists for auditing office accommodation

Note: The actions marked with a hash (#) may require specialist knowledge.

C.1 Temperature and humidity survey

Audit observations Check:

- incidence of thermal-related complaints (response to question 9 in questionnaire, Annex D) ☐
- recording instruments
  - calibration records ☐
  - accuracy ☐
- sensor settings ☐
- temperature records ☐
- humidity records ☐
- surfaces for signs of mould damage ☐
- surfaces for signs of mould growth ☐

Analysis of results Complete the analysis using information from the audit observations. If all the answers are 'yes', no further action needs to be taken. If any answer is 'no', go to *Action*.

	YES	NO
responses to question 9 in questionnaire less than 30%	☐	☐
recording instruments accurate	☐	☐
recorded values match specified values	☐	☐
no recorder but 'snapshot' readings deviate from specified values	☐	☐
surface free of moisture damage and mould growth	☐	☐

Action

- check design of thermal systems# (see Section 6) ☐
- check performance of thermal systems# (see Section 6) ☐
- check calibration of sensors# ☐

The IT Infrastructure Library
Maintaining a Quality Environment for IT - Auditing and Cleaning

	* install monitor(s)	☐
	* recommend remedial action#	☐

C.2 Air movement survey

Audit observations Check:

* incidence of complaints about air movement (response to question 11 in questionnaire, Annex D) ☐

* carry out preliminary smoke test using smoke tube ☐

Analysis If concern about draughts then:

Action

* carry out smoke test using smoke generator# ☐
* check influence of partitions# ☐
* check influences of cold surfaces# ☐
* measure air velocities at neck and ankle level and compare with standards# ☐

Analysis If deviation from specification/guidance then:

Action

* check air terminal selection# ☐
* check supply air temperature not too low# ☐
* check window fit ☐
* move occupants away from cold surfaces ☐

Analysis If concern about still air then:

Action

* check air supply system working as intended - eg all fans on ☐

* check for horizontal temperature variation (if there is inadequate air supply, temperatures may rise at locations away from supply air terminals, and local air changes may not meet design requirements - see Ventilation survey)# ☐

* check air terminal selection# ☐

Annex C
Checklists for auditing office accommodation

* check total throughput of air not below limit for air terminal devices or cooling requirement# ☐
* recommend remedial action# ☐

C.3 Air quality survey

Audit observations Check:

* cleaning logbook (See Annex F) ☐
* incidence of odour/dust related complaints (from questionnaire - question 12). ☐
* air filters
    - type (see Section 6) ☐
    - efficiency (see Section 6) ☐
    - maintenance records ☐
    - catching all polluted air ☐
* for evidence of air quality problems ☐
* with cleaners about any increase in dust levels ☐
* if any pollution sources have been identified indoors or near fresh air inlets, windows or doors ☐

Analysis of results Complete the analysis using the information from the audit observations. If all the answers are 'yes', no further action needs to be taken. If any answer is 'no', go to *Action*.

YES NO
* no evidence of odour/dust problems ☐ ☐
* air filters functioning properly ☐ ☐

Action If there is conclusive evidence that dust is a problem:

* identify source of dust
    - in room eg, printer, smoking ☐
    - in supply ducts ☐
    - in plenums ☐
    - in plant ☐
    - outdoors (inadequate filter installation?) (see Section 6) ☐
* recommend remedial action ☐

The IT Infrastructure Library
Maintaining a Quality Environment for IT - Auditing and Cleaning

If indicators are not conclusive:

* airborne dust monitoring may be required - seek specialist advice ☐

If odours are a problem and no obvious source is evident:

* arrange for thorough cleaning of all internal surfaces of the building and air distribution systems ☐

If problem persists after thorough clean:

* expert investigation may be required ☐
* undertake a ventilation survey (see below) ☐

C.4 Ventilation survey

Audit observations

Check:

* carbon dioxide concentrations in fully occupied space and hence estimate outdoor supply air rate# ☐
* for signs of short-circuiting using smoke tubes or smoke generator as appropriate# ☐

Analysis of results

Complete the analysis using information from the audit observations. If all the answers are 'yes', no further action needs to be taken. If any answer is 'no', go to *Action*.

	YES	NO
* measured values match specified values	☐	☐
* no evidence of short-circuiting	☐	☐

Action

If short circuiting identified:

* ventilation opening will require repositioning - seek specialist advice. ☐

If ventilation guidelines still not attained:

* increase outdoor air supply rate if possible - a check on plant thermal loading will be necessary# ☐

Annex C
Checklists for auditing office accommodation

C.5 Lighting and seeing conditions survey

Audit observations   Check:

* incidence of eye and head symptoms ☐
* incidence of complaints about screen ☐
* for screen reflections ☐
* image clear and stable ☐
* whether definition of letters is satisfactory, i.e. can the following be differentiated - X/K, O/Q, T/Y, S/5, I/1(one)/l, u/v, O/0(zero) ☐
* incidence of complaints about lighting levels ☐
* illuminance at working plane# ☐
* luminance range in field of vision# ☐

Analysis of results   Complete the analysis using information from the audit observations.. If all the answers are 'yes', no further action needs to be taken. If any answer is 'no', go to *Action*.

                                                                        YES NO
* low level of complaints   ☐   ☐
* lighting levels meet guidelines   ☐   ☐

Action

* recommend remedial action ☐

C.6 Workstation design survey

Audit observations   Check:

* that workstation assessment been carried out in compliance with legislative requirements ☐
* incidence of musculoskeletal complaints ☐
* incidence of complaints concerning furniture and space ☐

Analysis of results   Complete the analysis using information from the audit observations. If the answer is 'yes', no further action needs to be taken. If the answer is 'no', go to *Action*.

                                                                        YES NO
* workstation assessment carried out   ☐   ☐

The IT Infrastructure Library
Maintaining a Quality Environment for IT - Auditing and Cleaning

Action

* commission survey of workstation design (see also the CCTA/OHS guidance: Checklist for the Assessment and Analysis of Visual Display Screen Equipment Workstations). ☐

C.7 Noise survey

Audit observations   Check:

* incidence of complaints about excessive noise ☐
* for sources of noise and vibration ☐
* noise levels under various different conditions to identify influence of main sources# ☐

Analysis of results   Complete the analysis using information from the audit observations. If all the answers are 'yes', no further action needs to be taken. If any answer is 'no', go to *Action*.

                                                                                                                 YES NO

* low level of complaints ☐ ☐
* recorded values match guidelines ☐ ☐

Action

* recommend remedial action ☐

C.8 Electric and magnetic fields survey

Audit observations   Check:

* complaints about stability of visual display screen image (see C.5) ☐

Analysis of results   Complete the analysis using information from the audit observations. If the answer is 'yes', no further action needs to be taken. If the answer is 'no', go to *Action*.

                                                                                                                  YES NO

* visual display screens image stable ☐ ☐

Action

* investigate the possible causes ☐
* if necessary, carry out power-frequency field-strength measurements# ☐

Annex D. Model questionnaire

D.1 Management notes for running the questionnaire

*Note. This questionnaire may be incorporated as part of the workstation assessment under the **Health and Safety (Display Screen Equipment) Regulations**.*

Management should:

* inform staff that the questionnaire is being used as part of an ongoing programme of monitoring their working environment

* ask staff to fill it in whilst sitting in their normal working positions

* suggest that it should be filled in at the beginning or end of the working day (to prevent interruption)

* remind staff that questionnaires should represent individual opinions rather than a consensus

* attach to the questionnaire a simplified diagram of the working area, indicating that staff should mark the position at which they work for most of the time.

Discussion of the issues should be actively encouraged after completion of the questionnaire. To aid this, some feedback concerning the results should be circulated.

D.2 Management notes for analysis of questionnaire

The following points should be considered when analysing the questionnaires:

* positive responses may indicate potential problems (questions 9-19)

* calculate the percentage of positive responses for each question and for each category

* percentages of positive responses should be ranked

  - *5% or less* - probably does not present a problem overall, although some individuals may experience problems

- *5-30%* - represents a minority problem (maybe significant, but if from only one source may not require specialist examination)

- *30-40%* - significant minority problem, probably represents widespread concern (specialist knowledge required, high priority)

- *40% or more* - widespread problem, requires thorough investigation

* the questionnaire sections facilitate grouping of potential problems; for example, a high positive percentage in the **temperature and humidity** section as a whole, represents general concerns regarding the thermal environment.

* the floor plans showing the location of staff can be used to plot clusters of complaints which, for example, may indicate occurrence of problems connected with individual air-conditioning units.

D.3 Staff Questionnaire

The next four pages are formatted to allow their use as a free-standing questionnaire.

It should be stressed to staff completing the form that all answers will be treated confidentially.

Certain sections of the questionnaire relate directly to parts of Annex C as follows:

Temperature and humidity relates to Annex C.1

Air movement relates to Annex C.2

Air quality relates to Annex C.3

Noise relates to Annex C.7

Lighting relates to Annex C.5

Workstation design relates to Annex C.6.

Annex D
Model questionnaire

STAFF IN CONFIDENCE

On the last page you will find a diagram of the area where you work.
Please mark on this (with a tick) the area in which you work for most of the time.

About yourself

1. What is your job type?

    - Managerial ☐
    - Professional ☐
    - Technical ☐
    - Administration ☐
    - Clerical ☐
    - Other - Please specify

    [_____]

2. Are you   Male ☐   Female ☐

3. What is your age?

    - < 20 years ☐
    - 20-35 years ☐
    - 36-50 years ☐
    - > 50 years ☐

4. Do you wear spectacles at work?   Yes ☐   No ☐

5. Do you wear contact lenses at work?   Yes ☐   No ☐

6. Do you smoke at work?   Yes ☐   No ☐

7. Do you work in this building for 15 hours per week or more?   Yes ☐   No ☐

8. Are you classified as a display screen equipment 'user' under the HSE (Display Screen Equipment) Regulations?   Yes ☐   No ☐

STAFF IN CONFIDENCE

Page 1

The IT Infrastructure Library
Maintaining a Quality Environment for IT - Auditing and Cleaning

STAFF IN CONFIDENCE

Temperature and humidity

9. The temperature at your workstation

   Morning   Too high ☐   OK ☐   Too low ☐
   Afternoon Too high ☐   OK ☐   Too low ☐

10. The humidity at your workstation

    Morning   Too high ☐   OK ☐   Too low ☐
    Afternoon Too high ☐   OK ☐   Too low ☐

Air movement

11. The air at your workstation

    Morning   Too draughty ☐   OK ☐   Too still ☐
    Afternoon Too draughty ☐   OK ☐   Too still ☐

Air Quality

12. Are you troubled by odours at your workspace from:

    Tobacco smoke   Yes ☐   No ☐
    Other   Yes ☐   No ☐

    If 'yes', please specify
    [ ]

13. Are you troubled by dust at your workspace?   Yes ☐   No ☐

Noise

14. Are you disturbed by background noise as you work?   Yes ☐   No ☐

    If 'yes', please specify
    [ ]

15. Are you disturbed by background noise when you are talking or using the telephone?   Yes ☐   No ☐

    If 'yes', please specify
    [ ]

STAFF IN CONFIDENCE

Page 2

Annex D
Model questionnaire

STAFF IN CONFIDENCE

Lighting

16. Lighting levels at your desk

    Too high ☐   OK ☐   Too low ☐

17. Would you like more control over the level of lighting at your workstation?   Yes ☐   No ☐

18. Are you troubled by screen reflections from windows when viewed from your normal working position?   Yes ☐   No ☐

19. Are you troubled by screen reflections from interior lights when viewed from your normal working position?   Yes ☐   No ☐

Workstation design

20. Is your furniture suitable for your work?   Yes ☐   No ☐

Your health at work

Please tick any of the following symptoms if they bother you on a regular or frequent basis at work, but diminish or disappear when you leave the building:

21. Nasal symptoms eg. Irritation, runny noise, sneezing ☐
22. Eye symptoms eg. Itching, watering, eye fatigue ☐
23. Throat symptoms eg. Dryness, soreness ☐
24. Mouth symptoms eg. Dryness, nasty taste ☐
25. Skin symptoms eg. Dryness, rashes, irritation ☐
26. Chest symptoms eg. Breathlessness, tight, wheezing ☐
27. Musculoskeletal symptoms
    eg. Aching in back, neck, shoulder, arm, wrist, hand ☐
28. Head symptoms eg. Headache, tiredness, nausea, dizziness ☐
29. Flu-like symptoms eg. Shivering, fevers, aches ☐
30. Other symptoms
    - Please specify

STAFF IN CONFIDENCE

The IT Infrastructure Library
Maintaining a Quality Environment for IT - Auditing and Cleaning

STAFF IN CONFIDENCE

Work area

STAFF IN CONFIDENCE

Annex E. Checklists for auditing common services

Note: The actions marked with a hash (#) demand specialist skills which may not be available in-house.

E.1 Checklist for survey of air conditioning and air handling systems

E.1.1 Dust/mould related problems

Audit observations

Check:

* questionnaire (see Section 5.3) and results of any other environmental audits for any evidence that the air handling system could be a source of odour, dust and/or micro-organisms ☐

* air filters
    - maintenance records ☐
    - catching all polluted air ☐
    - general condition ☐

* internal condition of air handling plant for signs of
    - soiling of surfaces downstream of the filters ☐
    - mould, sludge and slime in condensate trays, in humidifier ponds, on drift eliminators, and on obstructions downstream of steam humidifiers ☐
    - pooling, rust and scale on surfaces downstream of cooling coils and humidifiers ☐
    - of rain penetration at outdoor air intakes ☐

Analysis of results

Complete the analysis using information from the audit observations.

If all the answers are 'yes', no further action needs to be taken. If any answer is 'no', go to *Action*.

	YES	NO
* air filters functioning properly	☐	☐
* do accessible sections of air distribution system (ductwork), in particular low velocity regions, appear clean	☐	☐
* is the air handling plant and distribution system downstream of filters clean	☐	☐

Action

* if access is impossible commission borescope survey# ☐
* review the filter installation and media specification ☐
* review the filter maintenance regime ☐
* clean internally the air handling plant and disinfect sites of microbiological growth ☐
* if necessary, clean internally the air distribution ductwork. ☐

E.1.2 Control checks

Audit observations   Check:

* results of other environmental audits ☐
* sensor
   - condition ☐
   - calibration records ☐
   - maintenance records ☐

Analysis of results   Complete the analysis using information from the audit observations. If all the answers are 'yes', no further action needs to be taken. If any answer is 'no', go to *Action*.

	YES	NO
* results of other environmental checks satisfactory	☐	☐
* sensor accuracy checked on regularly	☐	☐
* sensors in good condition	☐	☐

Action

* check that set points and proportional band widths are appropriate# ☐
* check accuracy of sensors in situ at various control settings# ☐

Annex E
Checklists for auditing common services

E.2 Checklist for water system audit

E.2.1 Audit of systems and equipment which pose a risk of legionellosis

Scope

Systems and equipment to be surveyed include:

* evaporative cooling towers and associated condenser water systems
* domestic hot water services systems and associated storage calorifiers
* tank cold water systems and associated storage tanks
* spray humidifiers
* indoor fountains
* base-exchange water softeners
* showers.

E.2.2 Checklist for audit to determine whether risk assessment satisfactory

Audit observations

Commission water sampling and analysis for general microbiological quality. Make sure the procedures below are followed, and ask laboratory for a full interpretation of results:

* sample areas
    - each cooling tower pond (most remote point from inlet or outlet) ☐
    - lowest point in cooling water system (if draw off cock provided) ☐
    - direct from each cold water storage tank (most remote point from inlet or outlet) ☐
    - direct from each storage calorifier ☐

The IT Infrastructure Library
Maintaining a Quality Environment for IT - Auditing and Cleaning

- draw-off from hot and cold water taps, one immediately after tap turned on, another after temperature has stabilized, as follows

    + furthest from storage ☐
    + least used ☐
    + closest to storage ☐
    + mains (baseline sample) ☐

* samples should be taken after a typical period of issue, e.g. before work starts on a Monday ☐

* temperatures for each sample should be recorded ☐

* sampling procedure should conform to **BS 6068 - Water quality: Part 6 - Sampling: Section 6.2 : 1991-Guidance on sampling** ☐

Analysis and action

If results of sampling indicate poor water quality, the cause of which is not obvious by inspection, a specialist investigation should be commissioned.

Audit observations

* check that all documentation is available, including report on risk assessment (see Appendix E.2.3) ☐

* inspect 'risk' systems and equipment (see Appendix E.2.1) ☐

Analysis

YES NO

* are there any elements (given in Annex E.2.3) not covered in the report on risk assessment? ☐ ☐

* have there been any changes which materially affect risk of legionellosis since the last risk assessment? ☐ ☐

    - water treatment regime has been altered ☐ ☐
    - equipment has been replaced or modified ☐ ☐
    - system has been extended or modified ☐ ☐
    - temporarily unused part of the system has been reinstated ☐ ☐

Annex E
Checklists for auditing common services

	- unplanned or emergency maintenance has been carried out ☐ ☐
	* are there signs of poor water quality or contamination of surfaces in contact with water? ☐ ☐
Action	If the answer to any of the above questions is 'yes', then:
	* commission a new risk assessment ☐
Audit observations	
	* examine maintenance and monitoring records ☐
Analysis	

                                                                                                                                                                              YES NO

* has water quality (microbiological and chemical) been outside acceptable limits, as specified by water treatment company? ☐ ☐

* have water storage and tap run-off temperatures been inside the risk range (20 to 50°C)? ☐ ☐

* was the last assessment carried out more than 12 months ago ☐ ☐

Action — If the answer to any of the above questions is 'yes', then:

    * commission a new risk assessment

N.B. Any unacceptable contamination, water quality problem or other risk factor must be dealt with at once and should not await the results of water sample analysis.

E.2.3 Checklist for a legionellosis assessment

Audit observations

* obtain documentation for all water systems

- drawings (scale layouts and schematics) ☐
- operating and maintenance instructions ☐
- maintenance logs since previous audit or last 18 months ☐
- reports on previous surveys and audits ☐
- report on risk assessment ☐
- health and safety policy statements ☐

The IT Infrastructure Library
Maintaining a Quality Environment for IT - Auditing and Cleaning

* inspect systems and identify risk of legionellosis
    - identify risk equipment ☐
    - identify design features which exacerbate risk ☐
    - observe condition of water and surfaces in contact with water ☐
    - identify potential pollution sources ☐
    - assess effectiveness of existing control measures ☐
    - assess effectiveness of existing maintenance regimes ☐
    - assess risk of control failure due to inadequate management or reporting ☐
    - assess competence of operating and maintenance personnel ☐

Analysis and actions Report on risk and identify remedial measures

The Approved Code of Practice (ACoP) requires that systems be reassessed when changes occur which affect the risk, for example when a system is modified or extended.

E.3 Checklist for audit of electrical installations

E.3.1 Introduction

All types of electrical equipment should be included in this audit whether energized or not. It also covers any conductors used to distribute electrical energy, such as cables, wires or leads.

This audit should check to ensure that a suitable and sufficient assessment of risk of electrocution, general health and safety or fire from electricity has been carried out in accordance with the **Electricity at Work Regulations 1989**.

Annex E
Checklists for auditing common services

E.3.2 Checklist for audit of compliance

Audit observations

* check that assessment of risk has been carried out and that all documentation is available showing conformity with **IEE Wiring Regulations, British Standards** and **Electricity at Work Regulations 1989** ☐

* carry out random/representative checks of electrical installations using the checklists given below# ☐

Analysis of results

* are there any concerns about: YES NO
    - electrical safety ☐ ☐
    - whether the assessment has been carried out properly ☐ ☐
    - whether the installation has changed since the assessment ☐ ☐

Action

If the answer to any of these questions is yes then:

* commission a full assessment of risk and preventive or protective measures ☐

E.3.3 Checklist for an electrical safety assessment

Scope

The checklist consists of three parts:

* prevention of electrocution
* general health and safety
* risk of fire due to electrical origin.

Audit observations

Prevention of electrocution

Check:

* that all electrical equipment, including connections, cables and fuses, is being used correctly, ie. within its load and operating tolerances, in accordance with manufacturers instructions# ☐

E 7

The IT Infrastructure Library
Maintaining a Quality Environment for IT - Auditing and Cleaning

* that the total load on the dedicated feeder cable is balanced across the phases within acceptable tolerances# ☐

* that any electrical equipment or cable that is damaged or showing signs of distress (such as overheating) is taken out of service at once to be examined by a competent person ☐

* that all electrical equipment undergoes a regular maintenance programme and that the frequency and adequacy of the inspections prevent all reasonable risk from danger ☐

* that all persons concerned with the operation, maintenance and testing of electrical systems are competent for the particular class of work undertaken# ☐

* that all materials expected to conduct electricity are either insulated or enclosed, preventing direct contact, or where this is not possible that there is adequate space to work, pass or retreat-into, around the electrical source# ☐

* that all conducting parts not normally live are prevented from becoming live, either by earthing, automatic disconnection or double insulation# ☐

* that all measures intended to cut off or limit the supply of electrical energy to any electrical equipment for safety reasons are suitably placed and function properly# ☐

* that any reports in log books of regular electrical difficulties have been investigated and remedied ☐

* that adequate power sockets are available and that multi-way adaptors are not being used ☐

General health and safety

Check:

* that all normal, supplementary and emergency lighting is working correctly and that unserviceable lamps have been replaced ☐

Annex E
Checklists for auditing common services

  * that there are no trailing leads or cables capable of causing a tripping hazard ☐

  * for incidence of electrostatic shock ☐

Risk of fire due to electrical origin

Check:

  * for overheating of cables or electrical equipment due to overloading of conductors# ☐

  * for leakage currents due to poor or inadequate insulation# ☐

  * that materials that may become flammable due to heat exposure are not placed too close to electrical equipment which may otherwise be considered to be operating normally ☐

  * that there is no flammable material present where electrical equipment can give rise to arcing or sparking ☐

  * (where the juxtapositioning of flammable materials and electrical equipment cannot be avoided) that the electrical equipment is of such construction or is so protected that the risk of fire is reasonably prevented# ☐

Analysis and action   Report on risk and identify remedial measures ☐

E.4 Checklist for compliance with fire protection legislation

E.4.1 Introduction

The following checklist has been compiled using **The guide to revised fire precautions law in fire certificated premises**. This guide is specially prepared to provide users of the Fire Safety Maintenance and Monitoring Manual with a sound working knowledge of the **Fire Precautions Act 1971**.

E.4.2 Certificate and Manual

Audit observations   Check:

  * that there is a current Fire Certificate ☐

The IT Infrastructure Library
Maintaining a Quality Environment for IT - Auditing and Cleaning

* that there is a comprehensive package of fire precautions in accordance with the certificate's specifications ☐

* that a "Responsible Person" within the premises has been given the responsibility to ensure that a consistent standard of fire precautions prevail ☐

* that there is a Fire Safety Maintenance and Monitoring Manual (referred to as the Manual from now on) for recording and monitoring compliance with current fire precaution requirements ☐

* that a system for keeping records and monitoring day to day fire precautions is operating and that all the required inspections are carried out and logged ☐

Analysis and action   Report any shortfall and identify remedial measures

E.4.3 Means of Escape

Audit observations   Check:

* that under the terms of the **Fire Precautions Act 1971**, the means of escape from the premises as specified on the Fire Certificate are not obstructed ☐

* that the means of escape are supported by, amongst other things, the installation of emergency lighting at strategic points and fixing of statutory fire safety signs, symbols and notices ☐

* to see if changes of conditions, particularly associated with building extension or alteration, have been recorded in the Manual after consultation with the Fire Authority ☐

Analysis and action   Report any risk and identify remedial measures ☐

E.4.4 Fire alarm systems

Audit observations   Check

* that the fire alarm system installed at the premises complies with **BS 5839 - Fire detection and alarm systems for buildings: Part 1: 1988 - Code of practice for systems** ☐

Annex E
Checklists for auditing common services

        design, installation and servicing, the procedures for which are listed in the Fire Safety Maintenance and Monitoring Manual

* that the specified inspections and tests are recorded in the relevant sections of the Manual i.e daily inspection of control panel, weekly fire alarm test etc   ☐

Analysis and action   Report on any shortfall and identify remedial measures

E.4.5 Automatic fire detection

Audit observations   Check to see if an automatic fire detection system has been installed   ☐

Analysis and action   If so then:

* check that the system is maintained to the requirements of **BS 5839: Part 1: 1988**, the procedures for which are listed in the Fire Safety Maintenance and Monitoring Manual   ☐

* check that details of all tests, checks, failures and maintenance etc, are recorded in the Manual   ☐

* report any deficiencies and identify remedial measures   ☐

If not, then:

* consider commissioning a feasibility study into installing such a system   ☐

* seek advice from the local Fire Officer   ☐

E.4.6 Electromagnetic door holders

Audit observations   Check to see if electromagnetic door holders have been fitted in the premises   ☐

Analysis and action   If so, then:

* check that they are all directly connected to the fire alarm system   ☐

* check that they have been tested in conjunction with the fire alarm system.   ☐

* check that the electromagnetic doors are functional by using the release button facility on each unit   ☐

* check that details of all tests, checks, failures and maintenance etc, are recorded in the Manual ☐

* report any deficiencies and identify remedial measurers ☐

If not, then:

* consider commissioning a review of the need for electromagnetic door holders ☐

* seek advice from local Fire Officer ☐

E.4.7 Emergency lighting system

Audit observations

Check to see if emergency lighting has been installed as is legally required (see also Annex E.3.2) ☐

Analysis and action

If so, then:

* check in the Manual to see if the emergency lighting system is discussed ☐

* check that the emergency lighting system has been designed adequately to illuminate

  - escape routes ☐
  - fire fighting equipment ☐
  - fire alarm call points ☐
  - changes of direction or levels ☐

* check that on the plan of the premises the positions of the luminaires and illuminated signs are referred to ☐

* check that the emergency lighting system is properly and regularly maintained to **BS 5266: Part 1: 1988: Code of practice for emergency lighting of premises other than cinemas and certain other specified premises used for entertainment** ☐

* check in the Manual that the monthly inspection of the system is recorded ☐

* report any deficiencies and identify remedial measures ☐

Annex E
Checklists for auditing common services

If not then:

* set up contract to design and install emergency lighting ☐

E.4.8 Portable fire extinguishing equipment

Audit observations

Check:

* Fire Certificate for the type, location and quantity of portable fire extinguishers in the building ☐

* that there is a system whereby every one employed in the premises is given instruction on the location and practical use of extinguishers ☐

* that the Responsible Person is aware of his/her duties for ensuring that all units are correctly maintained and replaced as necessary ☐

* on the building plan that all the portable fire extinguishers are marked using the correct symbols and abbreviations, and given a fire point number ☐

* that the provision and maintenance of the portable fire extinguishers meets the requirements of **BS 5306: Part 3: 1985: Code of practice for the selection, installation and maintenance of portable fire extinguishers**. ☐

Analysis and action

Report on any shortfall and identify remedial measures ☐

E.4.9 Employee fire safety instruction

Audit observations

Check:

* that as a legal obligation, there is a system in operation to ensure that all employees are provided with ongoing instruction and training in the procedure to adopt in the event of a fire ☐

E 13

The IT Infrastructure Library
Maintaining a Quality Environment for IT - Auditing and Cleaning

                              * that written instructions are issued to each employee and supported by periodic fire drill and that staff "fire action" notices are prominently displayed in the premises ☐

Analysis and action   Report any shortfall and identify remedial measures ☐

E.4.10 Periodic Fire Drills

Audit observations   Check:

    * that the number of fire drills to be held in one year is specified on the Fire Certificate ☐

    * that the details of each fire drill are recorded in the Manual, including dates, times, names of people missing and late arrivals ☐

    * that a reliable procedure for calling the fire service is in operation and outlined in the Manual ☐

Analysis and action   Report on any shortfall and identify remedial measures ☐

E.5 Checklist for audit of lightning protection system

Audit observations   Check to see if lightning protection system has been installed. ☐

Analysis and action   If so, then:

    * check that comprehensive records of lightning protection system, including logbook of inspection, testing and maintenance, are kept on site or by the person responsible for the upkeep of the installation; these records include ☐

        - documentary evidence that visual inspection of conductors, bonds and joints, and measurement of resistance to earth of the earth termination network and of each electrode are carried out by a competent person at regular intervals not exceeding twelve months to comply with **BS 6651: 1990 Protection of structures against lightning** ☐

        - documentary evidence that testing is carried out to the recommendations given in **CP 1013 Earthing** ☐

Annex E
Checklists for auditing common services

* during visual inspection pay particular attention to the following

    - earthing ☐

    - evidence of corrosion or conditions likely to lead to corrosion ☐

    - alterations or additions to the premises which may affect the lightning protection system ☐

* check that no part of a structure is protected in isolation ie there should be a fully interconnected lightning protection system ☐

* check that at each floor level provision is made for bonding future machinery or equipment to the lightning protection system as set out in the **IEE Regulations for Electrical Installations** ☐

    [PSA Standard Specification (M&E) No. 1 includes sections covering the components and installation of earthing and lightning protection systems.]

* identify any deficiencies and identify remedial action ☐

If not, then:

* commission an assessment of risk to property and people from lightning and its consequential effects, leading to commission of design and installation of a lightning protection system if a significant level of risk is established. ☐

Annex F. Cleaning of computer accommodation

F.1 Introduction

One of the main factors that affects the operation and reliability of computers is dust. Reducing the concentration of this pollutant is essential. Air conditioning systems are important in controlling airborne dust concentrations (see Sections 4.3.2 & 6.3.1) but even so the arrival of dust and dirt from all routes must be controlled. Therefore to maintain quality assurance in cleaning, it is important to provide a detailed specification which specifies:

* who is responsible for carrying out the tasks
* what tasks are to be carried out
* frequency of tasks to be carried out
* how tasks are to be carried out.

Cleaning should be carefully monitored against specifications.

Management role

The management role in the cleaning of computer accommodation is vital and a cleaning policy and specification should form part of an integral quality assurance programme. Cleaning must be coordinated and integrated with the overall engineering maintenance plan, and responsibilities for tasks clearly defined. Regular inspections should be carried out by supervisors.

See also the IT Infrastructure Library module **Computer Operations Management**.

F.2 Computer accommodation

F.2.1 Background

Depending on the design and age of the computer accommodation it should be possible to develop a cleaning policy and specification that minimises the amount of dust and dirt which finds its way onto surfaces and into equipment. Staff working time in the computer and media storage rooms should be limited, where possible. Many computer building designs now accommodate staff in a section adjacent to the main computer room sometimes known as the Computer Operations Room or Bridge.

The IT Infrastructure Library
Maintaining a Quality Environment for IT - Auditing and Cleaning

Simple precautions can be adopted to prevent dirt from entering the computer accommodation. Sticky floor pads at entrances together with the use of disposable plastic over-shoes can significantly reduce contamination. Clean overalls are essential for all maintenance staff entering the computer hall and maintenance equipment should also be kept clean.

Mainframe computer equipment is usually protected against contamination by in-built air filters. When these filters are changed the contaminated filters should be put into sealed bags immediately after removal.

If the air conditioning system fails, the recovery plan should contain a start-up and cleaning procedure. If dust has been allowed to accumulate in low velocity regions of the ductwork, it can be carried into the computer room when the air conditioning is re-started. To prevent this, ductwork and grilles should be regularly cleaned as part of the engineering maintenance procedure. Where the air conditioning system is normally in use all the time, the computer accommodation should be thoroughly cleaned as soon as possible before the equipment is re-commissioned. After that, weekly cleaning should be resumed.

Cleaning is essential at various stages of the construction and commissioning of new computer accommodation. Particulate air monitoring should be carried out to determine dust levels before and after the equipment is installed and commissioned and every twelve months after that (see Annex B.2). This will indicate the effectiveness of the filter installations and the cleaning services.

F.2.2 Cleaning specification

Responsibilities

Computer accommodation is often cleaned by staff from different departments or by a number of separate contractors. Normally maintenance engineers are responsible for cleaning:

* floor voids
* ceiling voids
* light fittings
* air grilles
* ductwork.

Annex F
Cleaning of computer accommodation

Cleaning staff or contractors will clean:

* walls
* floors
* surfaces.

Cleaning standards should be checked by cleaning shift leaders. Panels or covers must never be removed for cleaning without authority from the appropriate manager.

Daily tasks

* clean tape units and cleaner/evaluators
* vacuum clean all floor surfaces using central vacuum plant or portable equipment that meets the level of filtration set out in **BS 5415: Specification for vacuum cleaners wet and/or dry** and which is capable of removing particulate to a level of 95% efficiency at 5 micron
* dust wipe all surfaces up to 2 metres wall height (except computer equipment) using antistatic cloths
* remove stains or spots with a cloth which has been damp sprayed with antistatic cleaning fluid
* clean sticky antistatic mat at main entrance to computer room
* remove all waste products.

Weekly tasks

* where the computer room floor is covered in linoleum or PVC, lightly spray-buff the floor with antistatic floor treatment or a water based polish in sections; avoid contact with computer equipment. In the event of any uncertainty follow the polish manufacturers' recommendations.
* dust wipe all surfaces above two metres including luminaire diffusers and air terminal devices
* dust wipe the external cases and covers of computer equipment using a cloth which has been damp-sprayed with antistatic cleaning fluid.

Quarterly tasks

If the computer equipment can be powered down, switch off the air conditioning and ensure fire extinguishing system is switched to manual before removing floor or ceiling tiles.

If the computer equipment is in use for 24 hour per day this will not be possible:

* vacuum clean floor and ceiling voids in the following way

    - cover all equipment with antistatic dust sheets
    - remove each floor tile
    - wipe all surfaces, including stanchion, with an antistatic cloth
    - vacuum clean floor void using the central vacuum plant or a portable vacuum conforming to **BS 5415**

* remove (where possible) and wipe dust from inside luminaires and air terminal devices

* wipe dust from storage racks and associated equipment, under the supervision of computer staff

* change the sticky antistatic mat at entrance to computer room.

Half yearly tasks

* clean and reseal all PVC or linoleum floor coverings with a water-based seal, and buff floor.

Yearly tasks

* wash all surfaces using antistatic solution (except computer equipment)

* maintain and clean computer equipment in accordance with the manufacturer's recommendations. For computer equipment apart from PCs and terminals, cleaning is normally undertaken by the equipment's service contractor because of its specialist nature.

F.3 Office and ancillary accommodation

F.3.1 Background

When office or ancillary accommodation forms an integral part of the computer suite, identical cleaning and maintenance standards must be applied. If office areas are entirely separate then normal office cleaning procedures may be adopted. A specification for office cleaning is

Annex F
Cleaning of computer accommodation

included in the **Housekeeping Guide for Accommodation Managers** issued as a Department of the Environment guide. IT equipment requires special care.

F.3.2 Cleaning specification

Responsibilities

Cleaning staff are responsible for cleaning office and ancillary areas.

Staff using IT equipment should be suitably instructed on cleaning of this equipment. External surfaces of IT equipment can be cleaned using impregnated dusters or in the case of stains a damp cloth.

F.4 Cleaning audit checklist

When auditing cleaning, there is no substitute for direct inspection and for talking with cleaning staff. A general indicator of how well cleaning is being carried out is the tidiness of the area. Cleaning staff are unlikely to be able to clean desk and floor areas properly if they are untidy. For audit purposes it is important to know how many dust-related complaints are made. Records of complaints should be held in a cleaning log book for the computer department or for the office accommodation as a whole.

* examine dust related complaints from question 13 on the questionnaire (Annex D) ☐
* examine dust-related complaints from cleaning log-book ☐
* inspect documentary records of cleaning ☐
* inspect the accommodation for evidence of dust (preferably accompanied by the contract cleaning manager) ☐
* inspect the floor coverings ☐
* check that special precautions are being taken to prevent dirt being brought in by staff ☐
* check the cleaning cupboard to see that appropriate cleaning materials are being used ☐
* examine the cleaning equipment and check that electrical test certificates are up-to-date. ☐

Annex G. Environmental monitoring equipment

G.1 Introduction

This Annex provides outline specifications for equipment to be used for monitoring and auditing computer accommodation or offices where computers are used. An indication is given of where specialist training and knowledge is required to use the equipment. It is likely to be poor value for individual (IT) organizations to buy the same sophisticated instruments.

G.2 Thermal environment

The parameters that constitute a thermal comfort survey include:

* air temperature
* relative humidity
* radiant temperature
* air velocity.

It is possible to monitor all of these variables simultaneously using separate instruments or an indoor thermal climate analyser. All these units can be portable and self contained, and are relatively simple to use. Measurements can be undertaken by non-specialist staff if they are suitably trained beforehand, although the locations chosen for analysis and the duration of tests will need to be under the supervision of an experienced person. Interpretation of results may also require specialist knowledge.

Figure G1, overleaf, lists equipment that can be used for measuring aspects of the thermal environment.

G.3 Lighting

To measure light, an illuminance meter can be used. It should be calibrated in lux, with a range 0 - 10000 lux. Modern luxmeters are compact battery operated units with LCD displays and high precision photocells either integrated or linked to the meter.

Instrument	Aspects of thermal environment			
Description of Instrument	Air Temperature	Relative Humidity	Radiant Temperature	Air Velocity
Compact digital indicator LCD display 0.1% RH resolution - using moisture-sensitive transducer 0.1°C resolution - using heated thermistor	x	x		
Sling psychrometer (or whirling hygrometer) Wet and dry mercury in glass thermometers mounted in frame with swivel. Can be rotated to induce air currents	x	x		
Globe thermometer Mercury in glass thermometer, thermocouple or thermistor, with head at centre of matt black sphere			x	
Radiometer Measures flux density			x	
Anemometer Omnidirectional sensor Short time constant Accuracy of 0.05m/s				x

Figure G1: Equipment for measuring aspects of the thermal environment

G.4 Noise

To compare sound pressure levels within the workplace a sound level meter for dB(A) measurements with a range of approximately 25 - 130 dB will suffice. Commonly these meters are battery operated and have simple controls for ease of operation.

G.5 Dust monitoring

There are a number of ways of measuring airborne dust. Direct reading instruments are useful for identifying sources of dust and times of peak levels. However, these instruments require specialist handling and periodic calibration if they are to provide meaningful results.

Annex G
Environmental monitoring equipment

Instrument	Aspects of dust		
Description of Instrument	Particle sizing	Particle content	Concentration by mass
Dust measurement meter Uses radiation attenuation			x
Dust measurement meter Uses the piezo-electric technique			x
Dust measurement meter Uses light scattering technique	x	x	x
Gravimetric analysis Measures mass over a set period. Pump draws air sample through filter. Time-weighted average of dust concentration calculated from weight of dust and volume of air. Can also be used for personal exposure.			x

Figure G2: Equipment for measuring aspects of dust

A gravimetric technique can also be used to measure concentration by mass. Although this technique itself is relatively simple, the amount of dust collected is usually so small that a micro-balance with an accuracy down to 0.01mg is needed. Such balances are only found in specialist laboratories.

Figure G2 details equipment that can be used for measuring aspects of dust.

G.6 Gases and vapours, and ventilation

There is a wide range of equipment and methods for measuring the airborne concentrations of gases and vapours. Most of the direct reading instruments available are very sophisticated and expensive and need prior calibration. A good working knowledge of chemistry is also needed for the best results.

Alternatively, samples of the atmosphere can be taken and analyzed in a laboratory. Identifying the best sampling and analytical methods and equipment for a particular gas or vapour requires specialist knowledge.

The IT Infrastructure Library
Maintaining a Quality Environment for IT - Auditing and Cleaning

Air flow patterns can be determined in a number of ways. Good localized results can be obtained from equipment which is relatively cheap and simple to operate. However, detailed information of bulk air patterns will need specialist equipment.

Outdoor air supply rates can be determined using equipment that is again relatively cheap and easy to operate.

Figure G3 lists equipment that can be used for measuring aspects of gases, vapours and ventilation.

Instrument / Description of Instrument	Concentration of gas/vapour	CO_2 Concentration	Air flow patterns	Outdoor air supply rates
Direct reading instruments Range of technology incl: flame ionization detectors, infra-red and UV absorption detectors, colourimeters	x			
Colourimetric detector tube On-the-spot sampling of 200 gases. Air drawn through the tube - length of colour change gives gas/vapour concentration. Quick and easy results - not always accurate	x	x		
Sampling equipment Laboratory, specialist technique. Air is collected in special bags or bottles and drawn through tubes of absorbent material. Gas diffusion badges can also be used	x			
Smoke tube kit Enables visualization of localized flow patterns			x	
Commercial smoke generator			x	
Pitot tube and digital or inclined manometer For measurements within ductwork				x
Rotary vane anemometer				x

Figure G3: Instruments for measuring aspects of gases and vapours, and ventilation

Annex H. Model terms of reference for consultancy contracts

H.1 Introduction

The surveys which require specialist expertise should be planned in conjunction with the specialists themselves, who will need to be selected well in advance of the audit. The terms of reference should enable a judgement to be made on the grounds of quality as well as cost.

H.2 Selection of consultants

The chosen consultant should demonstrate the following characteristics, qualifications and experience:

* independence - consultants should not benefit from their recommendations; for example a consultant who surveys water systems should not also market water treatment chemicals or supply tank liners

* qualifications and experience - check that these are in areas relevant to the proposed surveys; ensure that CVs are obtained for the consultants who are going to be directly involved with the project

* quality assurance - if analytical work is required laboratories should ideally be NAMAS accredited and consultants should be QA certified to **BS 5750 Part 1: 1987** or **ISO 9001: 1987**; if not they should demonstrate that they are making progress towards reaching this goal.

H.3 Model terms of reference

H.3.1 Preamble

_____ (organization) is carrying out an audit of its computer accommodation and/or a building health check on its offices to ensure that:

* the environment is being maintained within design limits
* that all equipment is functioning as intended
* that legislative requirements are being met.

We therefore require the following surveys to be carried out:

Survey 1

Survey 2

etc.

(Give brief outline of each survey required, including:

* the parameters to be measured
* expected accuracy
* expected ranges
* sources for information.

Prospective consultants will be expected to obtain the relevant modules of the IT Infrastructure Library including this one and **Environmental Standards for Equipment Accommodation**)

H.3.2 Pre-qualification requirements

Pre-qualification requirements should include:

* previous similar experience - give brief case histories of relevant projects
* referees - give three previous clients for whom you have carried out similar work, complete with contact names, addresses and telephone numbers
* CVs of key consultants

Annex H
Model terms of reference for consultancy contracts

* approach or method statement - state your approach to this kind of work, detailing any specific area where your company has the advantage over others; give references, sample reports and other background material where appropriate

* give examples or details of any questionnaires, proformas, checklists, or analytical tools used in previous projects by your company

* equipment and laboratory facilities - list the main equipment you would use for this project and what arrangements you make for laboratory analysis, where appropriate

* QA - provide a review of your current quality management procedures; are you currently certificated? - give details

* professional indemnity - sum insured and policy details.

H.3.3 Scope

Following pre-qualification you would be expected to carry out the following as a minimum:

* site visit - sufficient information would be made available to enable the consultant to establish the full scale and nature of the works, including

  - layout
  - drawings
  - schematics
  - specifications
  - maintenance documentation
  - previous reports

* develop plan - you must develop an approach and programme to suit the specific needs and the nature of the project; a detailed statement is required, justifying the various elements in the quotation

* prepare quotation - quotations should be broken down into specific surveys and a time charge rate given for the various categories of staff employed, with an indication of the proportion of overall time allocated to each; the rules for tendering should be attached

* appointment
* carry out survey in liaison with site personnel
* report - 2 copies of a report should be submitted; the report should include
    - full details of the methods employed
    - results
    - interpretation and analysis
    - recommendations for remedial action
    - schedule of works indicating degree of urgency
    - budget costings for carrying out the works.

IT Infrastructure Library
Maintaining a Quality Environment for IT - Auditing and Cleaning

Comments sheet

CCTA hopes that you find this book both useful and interesting. We will welcome your comments and suggestions for improving it.

Please use this form or a photocopy, and continue on a further sheet if needed.

From:
                Name

           Organization

              Address

              Telephone

COVERAGE
Does the material cover your needs?
If not, then what additional material would you like included.

CLARITY
Are there any points which are unclear?
If yes, please detail where and why.

ACCURACY
Please give details of any inaccuracies found.

If more space is required for these or other comments, please continue overleaf.

IT Infrastructure Library
Maintaining a Quality Environment for IT - Auditing and Cleaning

OTHER COMMENTS

Return to: **Environmental Infrastructure Services**
CCTA
Riverwalk House
157 - 161 Millbank
LONDON SW1P 4RT

Further information

Further information on the contents of this module or other environmental books in this series may be obtained from:

CCTA
Environmental Infrastructure Services
Riverwalk House
157-161 Millbank
LONDON SW1P 4RT

Telephone: 071-217 3182 (GTN 217 3182).

Further information on the infrastructure management books in this series may be obtained from:

CCTA
IT Infrastructure Management Services
Gildengate House
Upper Green Lane
NORWICH NR3 1DW

Telephone: 0603 694854 (GTN 3014 4854).